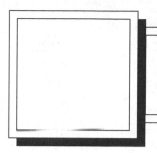

Classroom Management
for Secondary Teachers

Third Edition

Classroom Management for Secondary Teachers

Third Edition

EDMUND T. EMMER
The University of Texas, Austin

CAROLYN M. EVERTSON
Peabody College, Vanderbilt University

BARBARA S. CLEMENTS
Council of Chief State School Officers, Washington, D.C.

MURRAY E. WORSHAM
Northeast Independent School District, San Antonio, Texas

ALLYN AND BACON
Boston / London / Toronto / Sydney / Tokyo / Singapore

Copyright © 1994 by Allyn and Bacon
A Division of Simon & Schuster, Inc.
160 Gould Street
Needham Heights, MA 02194

Copyright © 1984, 1989 by Prentice Hall Inc.
A Division of Simon and Schuster, Inc.
Englewood Cliffs, New Jersey 07632

Editor-in-Chief, Education: Nancy Forsyth
Series Editorial Assistant: Christine Nelson
Production Administrator: Ann Greenberger
Editorial-Production Service: Progressive Typographers
Text Designer: Progressive Typographers
Cover Administrator: Linda Dickinson
Manufacturing Buyer: Louise Richardson
Composition Buyer: Linda Cox
Photo Researcher: Susan Duane

Library of Congress Cataloging-in-Publication Data
Classroom management for secondary teachers / Edmund T. Emmer . . .
    [et al.] — 3rd ed.
        p.   cm.
    Includes bibliographical references and index.
    ISBN 0–205–15490–5
    1. Classroom management. 2. Education, Secondary. I. Emmer,
Edmund T.
LB3013.C53   1993
371.1'024—dc20   93-1564
                                                         CIP

Printed in the United States of America
10 9 8 7 6 5 4 3 2 1   98 97 96 95 94 93

Chapter Opening Photo Credits: Chapters 1 and 5: Brian Smith
                    Chapters 2, 3, 4, 6, 7, 8, and 9: Stephen Marks

Contents

CHAPTER 3

Managing Student Work   **41**

CHAPTER 4

Getting Off to a Good Start   57

CHAPTER 5

Planning and Conducting Instruction   87

CHAPTER 6

Maintaining Appropriate Student Behavior — 113

CHAPTER 7

CHAPTER 8

Preface

The conventional wisdom about good classroom management is that no one notices it unless it's missing. Both new and experienced teachers recognize it as one of the most important foundations of good instruction. Yet good classroom management doesn't just happen. Smoothly running classrooms where students are highly involved exist because effective teachers have a clear idea of the types of classroom conditions and student behaviors that are necessary for a healthy learning environment. They not only have clear ideas, but they work very hard to create these conditions. This book describes what you can do to create a well-managed classroom. The process is described as teachers encounter it: first by planning in several key areas before the school year begins; then by implementing the plan and establishing good management at the beginning of the year; and finally, by maintaining the management procedures throughout the year. We have tried to make the material as useful and practical as possible by providing checklists to help you organize your planning. Several case studies and problem-solving scenarios are also provided that focus on critical areas that need special attention. We hope you will find much here that is helpful as you plan and organize for your own classroom.

This edition retains the same topics as the original book. The chapter on communication skills for teaching was added in the second edition and retained in this edition. One major change has been the addition of a new Chapter 8, "Managing Problem Behavior," which presents strategies you can use to restore order should it become necessary. Because not all misbehaviors are threats to your management system, this chapter helps you, first, to distinguish those behaviors that are minor from those that are serious and, second, suggests alternative strategies for dealing with them. Other changes are increased coverage of topics in several chapters, new case studies, and an updating of suggestions and recommendations to reflect current research in the field.

In writing this book, we have been influenced by our own experiences as teachers. In addition, much of our knowledge about classroom management derives from research and observation, both our own and others'. Our research program extends over twenty years and has included observational studies and field experiments in over 500 secondary and elementary classrooms. Data collected in this research are a major source of suggestions, guidelines, and case studies in this book. Therefore, we gratefully acknowledge our debt to the many teachers who permitted us to learn from them. Without this base of reality, this book would not exist. We are also grateful to Catherine H. Randolph for her editorial help on the revisions and to the many observers, school administrators, and other researchers who both assisted and enlightened us. The authors appreciate the suggestions of Barak Rosenshine for the organization and content of the section about clarity. We want to thank the following reviewers: Professor Melba Spooner, University of North Carolina/Charlotte; Professor Oscar Dorsey, Southwest Texas State University; and Professor Pharr.

1 Organizing Your Classroom and Materials

A logical starting point for classroom management is arranging the physical setting for teaching, because it is a task that you must complete before the school year begins. Many teachers find it easier to plan other aspects of classroom management after they have a clear idea of how the physical features of their classroom will be organized.

Good room arrangement can help you cope with the complex demands of teaching twenty-five to thirty or more students at a time for five or more periods a day. During any given period students will come and go, many activities will occur, and you and your class will use a variety of materials, texts, reference books, equipment, and supplies. Appropriate room preparation and arrangement of materials conserve class time for learning, while inadequate planning interferes with instruction by causing interruptions, delays, and dead time.

When you arrange the classroom, you will need to make many decisions. Should desks be set out in rows? Where should your desk be? What areas of the room will you use for presentations? How will you and the students obtain materials and supplies, and where will these be stored? This chapter will help you make these and other decisions about room arrangement. Each component will be described along with guidelines and examples to help you plan. In addition, a checklist for organizing your classroom, supplies, and equipment is provided. Use it to focus your efforts and to be certain that your classroom is ready for the beginning of school.

FIVE KEYS TO GOOD ROOM ARRANGEMENT

Remember that the classroom is the workspace for both you and your students. While it may hold as many as thirty or more students each period, it is not a very large area. Your students will be participating in a variety of activities and using different areas of the room, and they will need to enter and leave the room rapidly when classes change. You will get better results if you arrange your room to permit orderly movement, few distractions, and efficient use of available space. The following five keys will be helpful as guidelines when you make decisions about arranging your room.

1. **Use a room arrangement consistent with your instructional goals and activities.** You will need to think about the main types of instructional activities that will be used in your classes and then organize the seating, materials, and equipment compatibly. Thus, if your main activities will be teacher-led recitations, demonstrations, and presentations, students should be seated so that they can easily see the main instructional area, and you will need nearby storage space and surface for materials. If you plan extensive use of small work groups, however, you may need to arrange student seating and access to supplies quite differently.

2. **Keep high traffic areas free of congestion.** High traffic areas include group work areas, the space around the pencil sharpener and trash can, doorways, certain bookshelves and supply areas, student desks, and the teacher's desk. High traffic areas should be kept away from each other, have plenty of space, and be easily accessible.

3. **Be sure students are easily seen by the teacher.** Careful monitoring of students is a major management task. If the teacher cannot see all students, it will be difficult to identify when a student needs assistance or to prevent task avoidance or disruption. Therefore, clear lines of sight must be maintained between areas of the room that the teacher will frequent and student work areas.

4. **Keep frequently used teaching materials and student supplies readily accessible.** Easy access to and efficient storage of such materials and

Reprinted by permission: Tribune Media Services.

supplies will aid classroom management by allowing activities to begin and end promptly and by minimizing time spent getting ready and cleaning up.

5. **Be certain students can easily see instructional presentations and displays.** Be sure that the seating arrangements will allow all students to see the overhead projector screen or chalkboard without moving their chairs, turning their desks around, or craning their necks. Don't put your instructional area in a far corner of the room, away from a substantial number of students. Such conditions do not encourage students to pay attention, and they make it more difficult for students to take notes or copy material.

Each of the five keys presented will help produce good room arrangement. Some specific suggestions for achieving this goal are described below. By attending to these areas, you will address all the important aspects of room preparation. You can then be confident that you have designed a physical setting conducive to student involvement.

SUGGESTIONS FOR ARRANGING YOUR CLASSROOM

Bulletin Boards and Walls

Wall space and bulletin boards provide areas to display student work, instructionally relevant material, decorative items, assignments, rules, schedules, a clock, and other items of interest. Ceiling space can also be used to hang mobiles and other decorations. The following points should be considered when preparing these areas.

1. At the start of school, you should have at least the following displays for walls and chalkboards: a place for listing daily assignments and some

decorative display to catch your students' interest, such as a bulletin board with a "Welcome Back to School" motif or a display organized around a school-spirit theme ("Go Hippos!").

2. If you are teaching in a middle school or junior high school, or if you are teaching ninth graders in a senior high school, you should also reserve some wall or bulletin board space for posting classroom rules (at higher grade levels you might also post rules, or you might handle the communication of expectations orally and/or via a handout—see Chapters 2 and 4).

3. Other displays that many teachers find useful include an example of the correct paper heading to be used in your class and a content-relevant display such as one highlighting a topic that will soon be taught.

4. Covering large bulletin board areas with colored paper is an easy way to brighten your classroom. This paper comes on large rolls and is often kept in the school office or in a supply room. You can also trim the bulletin boards with an edging or border of corrugated paper. If you can't find these items in your supply room, consider spending a few dollars for these materials at a school supply center or variety store. You can also find books of bulletin board ideas as well as posters, cardboard punch-out letters, stencils, and other graphics for sale at such stores.

5. If you need ideas for decorating your room or for setting up displays, borrow some from other teachers. A look in some other rooms will probably give you several new ideas. Also, your departmental supply room may contain some instructionally relevant display material. Ask your department chairperson for assistance, if necessary.

6. *Don't* spend a lot of time decorating your room. You will have many other, more important things to do to get ready for the beginning of school. A few bare bulletin boards won't bother anybody. Leave one or two empty; you can add displays later or allow your homeroom/advisory students to decorate a blank space for an art project. You can also reward a "class of the month" with the privilege of redecorating a bulletin board. Finally, don't overdecorate your classroom. Wall space that is too filled up with detail can be distracting to the students; also, it makes a room seem smaller. It will seem small enough when all your students are in it.

Floor Space

Arrange your furniture and equipment so that you can easily observe students from all areas of the room in which you will work. Students should be able to see you as well as the overhead projector screen, the main chalkboard, and any other area that will be used for making presentations to the whole class. Of course, you will have to adjust to whatever constraints exist in your assigned classroom. A classroom may be too small or have inadequate or poorly located chalkboard space or electrical outlets. You should assess your space and determine whether any changes can be made to accommodate whatever constraints exist. For example, if the classroom is small, be sure to remove unnecessary student desks or extra furniture or equipment; if you have inadequate storage, perhaps you can locate an extra file or supply cabinet.

A good starting point for your floor plan is to locate where you will conduct whole-class instruction. Examine the room and identify where you will stand or work when you address the entire class to conduct lessons or give instructions. You can usually identify this area of the room by the location of a large chalkboard and the placement of the overhead projector screen. This area should also have space for a table or desk where you can place items needed in presentations and an electrical outlet for the overhead projector. Once you have located this area, you are ready to begin planning floor space.

As you read the following items, refer to Figure 1-1, which shows a well designed floor plan for a secondary school classroom in which whole-class

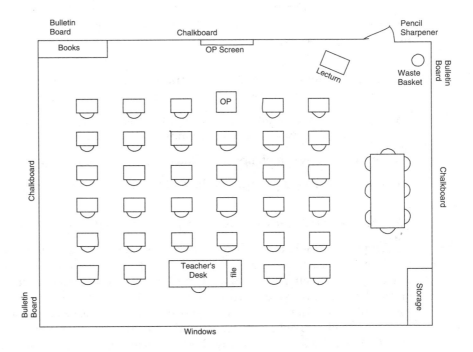

Figure 1-1 An Example of Good Room Arrangement for Whole-Class Instruction

instruction and individual seatwork are the main types of activities. Note how each item is addressed in this floor plan. Of course, this is just one of many possibilities. The location of desks, work areas, and other physical features of the classroom depends on the size and shape of the room and how different parts of the room will be used.

Arrangement of Student Desks

Many different arrangements of student desks are possible, but be sure to arrange them so that all students can look at the whole-group instruction area without having to get out of their seats. Also, avoid having students sit with their backs to the area. Try to avoid having students face potential sources of distraction such as windows, the doorway, an area where small groups of students will work, or eye-catching displays. Even if other arrangements are to be used later in the year, you might start the year with desks in rows facing the major instructional area. In such an arrangement students are less likely to distract each other than they would be if their desks were arranged in groups with students facing one another. In the example presented in Figure 1-1, the desks are arranged in rows, and no student is seated with his or her back to the major instructional area. Thus, if the teacher puts a display on the overhead projector screen, all the students can see it easily and take notes when necessary. The following items may also be of concern:

- Since it is important to keep high traffic areas clear, don't put desks or other furniture in front of doors, the pencil sharpener, sinks, and so on.
- Be sure to leave ample room around student desks so that you can easily approach students when you are monitoring seatwork activities.
- Count the desks or chairs and make sure you have enough.
- Replace damaged furniture or have it repaired.

The Teacher's Desk, Filing Cabinet, Overhead Projector, and Other Equipment

Your desk needs to be placed where it is functional. If you intend to keep at your desk instructional materials used during presentations, the desk should be adjacent to the main instructional area or areas. If you plan to work at your desk at any time during the day, you will need to locate your desk to facilitate monitoring: Sit facing the students and be sure you can observe all of them from your seat. However, it is not necessary that students be able to see you from their seats, and some teachers prefer placing their desks at the back of the room rather than at the front (Figure 1-1). If you plan to work with individual students at your desk, you will also have to consider traffic patterns near your desk. Student desks should not be so close to yours that students will be distracted by other students approaching your desk or working with you there.

Other furniture, such as the filing cabinet and storage bins, needs to be located where it is functional. An item used for storing seldom used supplies can be safely tucked away in a corner or hidden out of view. Supplies that will be used frequently during class should be located near the area in which they will be used. All electrical equipment must, of course, be placed near an outlet and covered or otherwise secured.

Bookcases

These should be placed where they will neither prevent your monitoring students nor obstruct students' ability to see chalkboards or relevant displays. If a bookcase contains items that are to be used frequently, such as dictionaries or supplemental texts, it needs to be conveniently located and easily monitored. If a bookcase is used to store seldom used items, an out-of-the-way place is best. If you have only one bookcase, store unneeded items in a cabinet so that the single bookcase can be used for materials in frequent use.

Work Areas

In many subjects, such as science, industrial arts, homemaking, or art, students may spend part of their time in a laboratory, shop, or other work area. The area may be in the same room or in another room adjacent to the classroom. Students may work individually or in groups. Students may also work in small groups for discussion activities or for special projects in other subject areas as well. When arranging group work or laboratory areas, follow the same principles you used when positioning student desks. Be sure you can see all students, keep traffic lanes clear, and avoid congested areas, especially near supply and cleanup areas. Provide clear lines of sight between students and any area of the room from which you will conduct instruction while students are in the work area.

Centers

A center is an area where a few students come to work on a special activity or to study some topic. Often a center will have special equipment, such as a tape recorder with headphones, for individual students. Other centers may be organized around a special study topic or around skill areas in a particular subject. In the latter case, the teacher might have a box of activity cards that students use to progress through a series of objectives as part of enrichment or remediation programs. It is important to note that you do not need to have a center in your room, particularly at the beginning of the school year. There will be time enough later to introduce this feature into your classes if you so desire. If and when you do use a center, be sure to place it in a location where you can monitor students easily. Also, be certain that all necessary materials and equipment are available at the center and work properly.

Pets, Plants, Aquariums, and Special Items

These can add interest and individuality to a room. However, the first week of school is already quite exciting for students, so it is not necessary to introduce these special features immediately. When you do bring in such items, place them where they won't be distracting, especially during whole-class activities. Of course, they should not impede movement about the room nor interfere with students' work activities.

Storage Space and Supplies

Once you have decided on your wall and bulletin board displays and have organized space within the classroom, you can concentrate on obtaining supplies and providing for storage. Some supplies will be used frequently and thus will need to be readily accessible. Other items will be seasonal or infrequently used and can go into deeper storage.

Textbooks and Other Instructional Materials

You need to identify the textbooks and supplemental materials (dictionaries, reference books, supplemental reading materials) that will be used in your class. Determine which books the students are expected to keep in their possession and which must remain in the room. Then find easily accessible shelves in a bookcase for those everyday books and materials that will not be kept by students. If you do not know what supplemental materials are available or what the school policies are regarding these items, check with your department chairperson, with the librarian, or with another teacher. Also, find out what system is used for obtaining textbooks; often it is first come, first served. If so, get in line early to ensure that you obtain the books you need.

Frequently Used Classroom Materials

These are supplies that you and your students will use; the necessary items will depend somewhat on the subject you teach. A basic set includes paper in varying sizes and colors, water-soluble markers, rulers, scissors, chalk and erasers, transparent tape and masking tape, stapler, and glue. Other than the chalk kept in the chalk trays, these and any other supplies you need on a daily basis should be kept in a readily accessible place, such as on a worktable or shelf. Usually students are expected to supply certain materials, including pencils, erasers, pens, and notebook paper or spiral notebooks. Since you cannot expect that all students will bring these materials at the beginning of the year, you should make sure you have an ample supply of items needed by students. It is also a good idea to give parents a list of supplies that students will need in your class.

Teacher's Supplies

You will receive some materials from the school office for your own use. These items, which usually should be stored in your desk, include pencils and pens, paper, extra chalk, overhead transparency sheets, scissors, ruler, stapler, file folders, paper clips, and thumbtacks. In addition, you should receive a grade book, a lesson plan book, teachers' editions for all textbooks, and any forms or tablets needed for attendance reports and for handling money. Set up a filing system that allows you to separate the notes, forms, papers, and other materials used in each class. Use different file folders for different periods and color code them for added efficiency. For each period, keep frequently needed materials and forms separate from those needed only occasionally.

Other Materials

In addition to the items supplied by the school, a number of other supplies will come in handy. If your room does not have a clock and a calendar, obtain these now. Both should be large enough to be seen from all areas of the room. You may wish to buy a desk bell or a timer if you are going to use these as signals for starting or stopping activities. You might also add the following items: tissues, rags or paper towels, a bar of soap, bandages, scouring powder or liquid cleanser, and a small plastic bucket. Some teachers like to keep a few basic tools such as a hammer, pliers, and screwdriver in case a minor repair needs to be made. Store all these items where they are accessible to you but not to your students.

Equipment

Check all equipment, including the overhead projector, record player, tape recorder, headphones, pencil sharpener, and so on, to make sure they are in working order. Get any necessary extension cords or adapter plugs and store these either with the equipment or in a handy place.

Seasonal or Infrequently Used Items

This category includes Halloween, Thanksgiving, and Christmas items as well as other seasonal decorations, bulletin board displays, or special project materials. Also included are instructional materials that are used only on some occasions, for example, compasses and protractors, templates, special art materials, science equipment, and so on. Because you don't need to have ready access to these materials, you can store them at the backs of closets, in boxes on top of cabinets, or even out of the room if you have access to outside storage space. Check with your department chairperson about using a storeroom.

Special Project Materials

In a few subject areas, such as industrial arts, homemaking, or art, students may regularly work on projects. Occasionally these projects may become bulky or awkward to store in lockers and must remain in the room. You will need to provide special storage areas to which you can control access to safeguard the materials. You will be wise to avoid beginning such projects until you have arranged for adequate storage.

"Come now, Miss Twist, your class isn't *that* large!"

IF YOU HAVE TO "FLOAT"

At some time in their careers, many teachers have to share classrooms with other teachers. Sometimes teachers who are new to a school find that they have no classroom that they can call their own but instead have to "float," conducting their classes in three or more rooms during the day. Obviously, such a situation presents some problems for classroom organization and management. If this is the situation you face, your ability to arrange and organize your classroom space the way you would like will be very limited. However, there are some things you can and should do before school begins.

First, confer with the other teachers whose classrooms you will be using. Inspect each room carefully so that you will know where everything is when school begins. In each room try to arrange for the following:

- An overhead projector in place for daily use. This is practically a must. You will not have the time—and you may not have the space—to put lessons, assignments, notices, and so on, on the chalkboards each period. You can save yourself much effort by preparing ahead of time transparencies to use in each of your classes. Also, you can use blank transparency sheets to write on as you would a chalkboard during lesson presentations. (Another advantage of using transparencies instead of chalkboards in borrowed classrooms is that they provide you with a record of what you presented to your students.)

- A regular space on the chalkboard or on a bulletin board where you can post assignments or announcements for your class and leave them up for a week or more.

- One shelf, cabinet, or table, especially if your course requires a classroom set of materials that you cannot carry around with you all day.

- A sufficient number of desks.

Either plan to carry all essential teaching supplies with you each day or store them in one desk drawer or in a box in each room. Don't depend on other teachers for supplies. You will probably need transparency sheets and markers, water and paper towels, chalk, extra pens and pencils, paper, paper clips, and tissues. File folders, large manilla envelopes, and rubber bands will be useful for organizing and carrying student papers. Color coding folders for each class will also help.

If all of your classes are on one floor, try to obtain a rolling audiovisual cart. A large sheet of tagboard taped to the front will provide bulletin board space and also a little bit of privacy for your belongings. Think about assigning early arriving students the task of preparing the room (e.g., erasing boards, arranging chairs, or positioning the projector).

SUGGESTED ACTIVITIES

The following activities will help you plan and organize your classroom space. Do as many of them as you have time for.

1. The drawing in Figure 1-2 shows a classroom with quite a few problems. See how many you can find and consider how each problem might be corrected. (A key for this activity is found in the Appendix.)

2. Two other room diagrams are shown in Figure 1-3. Discuss their advantages and disadvantages for different types of classes. With which keys are they consistent or inconsistent? Would any rearrangements be helpful?

3. Make a scale drawing of your room, as in Figures 1-1 and 1-2. You can now experiment on paper with different furniture arrangements and the organization of space—a much simpler task than pushing the furniture around yourself. Try to evaluate your arrangement, using the five keys to successful room arrangement presented earlier in the chapter.

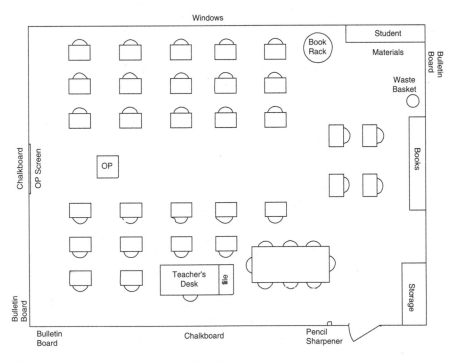

Figure 1-2 A Room Arrangement with Problems

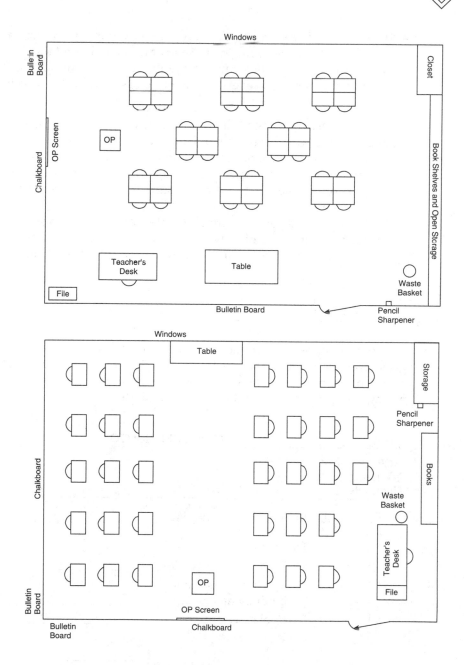

Figure 1-3 Two Room Arrangements for Discussion

4. Visit some other teachers' classrooms and examine their room arrangements. Use the items in Checklist 1 at the end of the chapter and the five keys to room arrangement to guide your observation and analysis. If you are having a specific problem, ask several teachers for suggestions and see how they may have coped with the same problem.

5. After you have arranged the furniture in your room, test the traffic patterns, keeping in mind the recommendations in this chapter.
   a. Go to each instructional area and check it for your ability to observe all students wherever they may be during the instructional activity in that portion of the room. Also, be sure that needed materials are readily accessible.
   b. Now pretend you are a student. Enter the room; go to several desks; check for visibility, ease of movement to other parts of the room, and possible distractions. Alter the arrangement if you detect problems.

CHECKLIST 1

To organize and keep track of your activities as you arrange your room and get supplies and equipment ready, you will find it helpful to use Checklist 1. Each aspect of room arrangement has been listed, and space has been provided for noting things to be done and for checking off the area, once you have it ready.

ROOM PREPARATION

Check When Complete	Subject	Notes
☐	A. Bulletin Boards and Walls	_____
	B. Floor Space	
☐	1. Student desks/tables	_____
☐	2. Teacher's desks and equipment	_____
☐	3. Bookcases	_____
☐	4. Work areas	_____
☐	5. Centers	_____
☐	6. Pets and plants	_____

Check When Complete		Subject	Notes
	C.	Storage Space and Supplies	
☐		1. Textbooks	_____
☐		2. Frequently used instructional materials	_____
☐		3. Teacher's supplies	_____
☐		4. Other materials	_____
☐		5. Equipment	_____
☐		6. Seasonal items	_____
☐		7. Special project materials	_____

Choosing Rules and Procedures

Good classroom management is based on students' understanding what behaviors are expected of them. A carefully planned system of rules and procedures makes it easier for you to communicate your expectations to students. It also helps ensure that the procedures you set up will be workable and appropriate. The goal of this chapter is to help you identify a good system of rules and procedures for your classes.

PRELIMINARY CONSIDERATIONS

Rules and procedures vary in different classrooms, but all effectively managed classrooms have them. It is just not possible for a teacher to conduct instruction or for students to work productively if they have no guidelines for how to behave or when to move about the room, or if they frequently interrupt the teacher and one another. Furthermore, inefficient procedures and the absence of routines for common aspects of classroom life such as taking and reporting attendance, turning in materials, or checking work can waste large amounts of time and cause students' attention and interest to wane. A brief example of a classroom with major problems in the area of rules and procedures is presented below.

> When the tardy bell rang, only a few of Mr. Smith's third-period students took their seats. Two played catch with the erasers, while others congregated in small groups and chatted noisily. Mr. Smith had to shout over the din in order to be heard: "Get to your seats. I need to take roll." Some students moved to sit down, while others vied for places at back-row desks. After much prompting, most of the students were seated and Mr. Smith began taking roll. Loud talking continued, abating only momentarily after Mr. Smith called repeatedly for silence. After ten minutes roll call was finally completed. Mr. Smith then asked students to get out their books and homework assignment. Loud protests ensued as students insisted that no assignment had been given. Furthermore, many students did not have their textbooks with them. Rather than allow a large number of students in the hallways to retrieve their books from their lockers, Mr. Smith decided to conduct a recitation on the assigned lesson. However, by then three students had already left the classroom to retrieve their texts. Attempting to get the recitation underway, Mr. Smith called in vain for silence. He finally began to ask questions, but before he could select a student to respond, several others called out the answer. A chorus of comments greeted the responses. Mr. Smith tried to continue asking questions, but the noise from students' social talk made it difficult to hear. Soon paper airplanes began to drift through the air. . . .

Observers of this classroom might criticize Mr. Smith for allowing students to get away with so much misbehavior. "Be stricter," they might say. "Punish the misbehaving students." Or "Develop more interesting lessons to capture student interest." Some might even suggest that Mr. Smith set up a reward system to encourage good behavior. While these suggestions could be helpful under some circumstances, they do not address the fundamental problem in this classroom: The students have not learned the behaviors that are expected of them. These students almost certainly know that many of their behaviors would not be allowed in other classrooms, but the problem is that Mr. Smith has not taught the students how to behave in his class. Areas in which this is evident in this example include (1) what to do upon entering the room, (2) behavior during roll call, (3) bringing materials for class, (4) completing assignments, (5) out-of-room policies, (6) talking during discussions, (7) responding to questions, and (8) seating assignments.

Of course, just knowing what is appropriate does not mean that students will behave that way. (For that reason, this book will not end with the present chapter!) However, a clear set of expectations of what constitutes appropriate behavior will be a major start toward establishing a well-managed classroom environment.

Finally, remember that the unique setting created by secondary school organization makes it essential that you establish a clear set of rules and procedures for your classroom. You will need to work with five or more groups of twenty-five to thirty or more students every day. Generally you will be confined to a single room with limited space and materials; you will be responsible for teaching many cognitive skills to a diverse population of students; and at the same time, you will have to handle administrative tasks, arrange for appropriate materials and supplies, and evaluate students. In order to do these things well, you and your students need an orderly environment with minimal disruption and wasted time, leaving everyone free to concentrate on the critical tasks of learning. Carefully planned procedures help create this environment.

Definition of Terms

Rules and *procedures* each refer to stated expectations regarding behavior. A rule identifies general expectations or standards. For example, the rule "Respect other persons and their property" covers a large set of behaviors that should always be practiced. Rules frequently indicate behavior that is not acceptable, although teachers sometimes manage to write only rules that are positively stated

© 1968 by Bill Knowlton. Reprinted from *Classroom Chuckles* published by Scholastic Book Services.

(for example, "You may talk when given permission"). In such instances the unacceptable behavior is implied (that is, "Don't talk without permission"). In addition to general rules, many teachers will have a rule or two governing a specific behavior they anticipate being an issue or that they want to prevent (for example, "No profanity" or "Gum chewing is not allowed").

Procedures also communicate expectations for behavior. They usually apply to a specific activity, and they are usually directed at accomplishing something rather than at prohibiting some behavior or defining a general standard. For example, you will set up procedures with your students for collecting assignments, turning in late work, participating in class discussions, leaving the room to go to lockers or the bathroom, and so on. Some procedures, such as safety practices for a laboratory or for equipment use or student notebook requirements, may be sufficiently complex or critical that you should provide duplicate copies of guidelines for students to retain, or you may have students copy the procedures into their notebooks. However, many procedures are not written, either because they are very simple or because their specificity and frequency of use allow students to learn them rapidly.

Identifying School Rules and Procedures

In most schools teachers are expected to enforce school rules. It is to your advantage to do so. A set of rules applied consistently in all classes and areas of the building is easy for students to learn. The rules also acquire more legitimacy in the eyes of some students because the rules are everyone's rules. In addition to rules and procedures that regulate student behavior, all schools have certain administrative procedures which must be followed by every teacher (for example, keeping attendance records). You need to find out about your school's rules and procedures before the year begins so that you can also incorporate them into your own classroom procedures. You can find out about school rules for students and administrative procedures for teachers at a school orientation meeting or from a teacher's handbook, a building administrator, or another teacher. Pay careful attention to the following:

1. Behaviors that are specifically forbidden (for example, running in the halls, possession of particular items) or required (for example, being in possession of a hall permit when out of the classroom during class time; bringing a note for absence).

2. Consequences of rule violations. In particular, you need to note the responsibility you have for carrying out the consequences, such as reporting the student to the school office. If the school does not have a policy for

dealing with certain rule violations, check with other teachers to learn about school norms. For example, if it is up to the teacher to deal with the issue of coming late to class, you need to be ready with a system.

3. Administrative procedures that must be handled during class time. These procedures include beginning-of-year tasks, such as assigning textbooks to students, collecting fees, and checking class rosters. Fee collection may go on all year, so you'll need some system of record keeping and a safe place to keep the money until you can turn it in to the school office. Some administrative tasks will need to be conducted each class period. These include taking and recording class attendance in your grade book, handling previously absent students, and filing an attendance report with the office. You will also need a procedure for tardy students and for allowing students to leave the room once the period begins (not that you'll encourage it). Frequently procedures in these areas will already be established for the school. If uniform procedures have not been adopted in some area, talking with some experienced teachers about their procedures should be helpful.

Planning Your Classroom Rules

Once you have information about school rules and procedures, you will be ready to begin planning for your own classroom. Guidelines for rules will be presented separately from procedures.

Many different rules are possible, but a set of five to eight rules should be sufficient to cover most important areas of behavior. Six general rules that encompass many classroom behaviors are listed below. These or similar rules are often found in well-managed classrooms, although we do not present them as a definitive list. You may decide to use other rules (for example, a rule prohibiting a specific behavior) or different wording. For some teachers these rules might be too general, and these teachers might like to have more rules with greater specificity. After each rule are examples of behaviors related to the rule. When presenting general rules to students, it is important to discuss your specific expectations relevant to each rule. During the discussion of the rules and related behaviors, it is best to emphasize the positive "do" parts of the rules rather than just their negative counterparts. When you do the former, you help students learn how to behave appropriately. You will need to be explicit about behaviors that are not acceptable when such behaviors might occur frequently (for example, gum chewing, leaving one's seat, calling out). These may be incorporated into your set of rules or discussed when presenting procedures associated with specific activities. However, there is no need to recite a long list of forbidden behaviors during your initial discussion of rules.

The set of rules you choose will be used later in several ways. First, you will discuss these rules with your students on the first day or two of class. If you teach at the junior high or middle school level, you will also post the rules in the room and/or make certain that students have their own copies. You might also send a copy home to be returned with parents' signatures. A posted set of rules allows you to focus student attention on and create a strong expectation about behaviors that are very important to you. If you teach in a senior high school, posting rules is not mandatory, although it is definitely recommended for ninth-grade classes; these students will be less aware than older students of what behaviors are appropriate for the high school setting. At higher grade levels you can provide students with a handout describing class rules, along with other information about the class. There is also some difference in how you should present the classroom rules to younger and older students, but this will be described in Chapter 4. Finally, you may refer to specific rules as needed to remind students of appropriate behavior during the year. It should be noted that your posted rules need not (and cannot) cover all aspects of behavior in detail. Procedures for specific activities and perhaps some ad hoc rules will be needed. For instance, you may wish to keep your policies regarding student work separate from rules about general conduct. Examples of some commonly used, basic rules are presented below.

RULE 1. BRING ALL NEEDED MATERIALS TO CLASS.   This rule can be helpful because it emphasizes that students must be prepared for each class period. It is important for students to know exactly what they are expected to bring to class in order for this rule to be followed. Thus, students should know whether to bring a pen or pencil, paper, notebook or folder; and if more than one textbook is used in the class, which textbook. If the materials vary (such as a notebook being required on one day but not another), then some system will be needed to signal this to students. If possible in such cases, the teacher should develop a routine such as having students bring certain materials on particular days of the week (for example, spelling books on Thursday) or having students copy into their notebooks on Monday a list of materials needed for each day that week.

RULE 2. BE IN YOUR SEAT AND READY TO WORK WHEN THE BELL RINGS. Included under this rule may be procedures such as: (a) pencils should be sharpened before the bell rings; (b) paper and pens should be out and ready for work (including heading); and (c) warmups or other opening activities are to be started as soon as possible after entering the room.

RULE 3. RESPECT AND BE POLITE TO ALL PEOPLE.   Included under this rule are listening carefully when the teacher or a student is speaking, and behaving properly for a substitute teacher. Some "don'ts" include fighting, name calling, bothering, and so on.

RULE 4. LISTEN AND STAY SEATED WHEN SOMEONE IS TALKING. This rule addresses two student behaviors that, if unregulated, can become sources of widespread misconduct. Rule 4 is actually a more specific but less inclusive variation of rule 3. Because it is clearly stated, the rule requires little interpretation for students to understand it.

RULE 5. RESPECT OTHER PEOPLE'S PROPERTY. This rule may include guidelines such as: (a) keep the room clean and neat; (b) pick up litter; (c) return borrowed property; (d) do not write on the desks; and (e) get permission before using another person's materials.

RULE 6. OBEY ALL SCHOOL RULES. This is a useful rule to include because it reminds students that school rules apply in your classroom as well as out of it. It also suggests that you will monitor behavior in the areas covered by the school rules. Finally, including it in your rules gives you an opportunity to discuss whatever school rules are pertinent to your classroom.

Student Participation in Rule Setting

Some teachers involve students in rule setting in order to promote student ownership of the rules and more student responsibility for their own behavior. Student involvement can take many forms, such as a discussion of reasons for having rules and clarifying the rationale for and the meaning of particular rules. For example, a discussion might begin with the teacher making an analogy between society's laws and classroom rules and asking students what purpose these laws serve. Depending upon the age level and sophistication of the students, typical responses might include ideas about protecting individuals and group rights, preventing violence or destructive behavior, and permitting normal activities to take place. After this initial discussion, rules can be presented one at a time. The teacher may first clarify the rule by describing (or asking students to describe) the area of behavior it covers. Students can usually supply concrete examples, although they will tend to give negative instances (for example, "Respecting property means not marking up desks or not stealing"). Consequently, you should be prepared to encourage students to state some positive examples. The discussion of individual rules should also include a rationale for those rules whose justification is not obvious.

Another way of involving students in rule setting is to allow them to share in the decision-making process for specific rules. This is sometimes done at a school level by having student representatives or student council members participate in the identification of school rules. However, shared decision making is not commonplace in secondary classrooms for several reasons. First, the domain in which student participation is acceptable is limited. Schoolwide rules must be accepted as they are. Also, policies that are essential to managing instruction cannot be left to student discretion. Finally, it must be remembered that secondary school teachers instruct five or more classes. If each class generates different rules, posting them may be a problem and remembering which rules are associated with which class may become cumbersome.

Some teachers limit student choice to particular activities or behaviors. For example, if gum chewing is not prohibited by a school rule, and if you do not find it objectionable, you could give your students a choice. It would be a rare class that decided to prohibit it! Another area in which an option may be available concerns whether seatwork is to be done silently or whether quiet talking is acceptable. When students are given such choices, you must also make them aware of their responsibility for making the chosen procedure or rule work and remind them that they will lose the privilege if their behavior warrants it.

It is important to note that many effective managers do not provide for student choice in rule setting. Instead, they clearly present their rules and procedures to students and provide explanations of the need for such rules. These teachers strive to be reasonable and fair in their rules and procedures: Teachers who act autocratically invite challenges from adolescents. However, a teacher who is authoritative, who establishes reasonable rules and procedures, who provides an understandable rationale for them, and who enforces them consistently will find the great majority of students willing to abide by them.

Consequences for Rule Violations

You should give careful consideration to consequences for violations of your rules. One type of consequence is usually prescribed by school policy, such as consequences for tardiness and unexcused absences. Other consequences are often specified for fighting, classroom use of profanity, and damage to property, and loss of books. You will need to familiarize yourself with these policies, to do your part in following through if rules violations occur and to be sure that your own classroom policies are consistent with the school's. You will also need to consider what other consequences you will use to deal with classroom rules that aren't covered by school policy. For example, what will you do if a student ignores your rule for respecting others and chooses to interrupt your lessons by walking around the room to visit with friends? What consequence will you use if a student turns in an incomplete assignment? Planning consequences ahead of time is a good idea because it helps you use them consistently, and you will be more confident about using them. Also, you will be better able to communicate them to students. Ideas for consequences, including many alternatives applicable to different types of problems, can be found in Chapters 6 and 7, so we will not elaborate on the topic at this time.

Planning Classroom Procedures

If you have never analyzed the specific behaviors required of students in a typical secondary school classroom, you are going to be surprised by the complexity and detail in the following sections. Do not hurry through them, even though some of the items may appear trivial. These bits and pieces will combine to form the mosaic of your management system. Four categories of procedures are described: general procedures needed each class period, procedures for teacher-led instruction and seatwork activities, procedures for student group work, and miscellaneous procedures. The greatest emphasis is on the first two areas, although the third is very important, should you plan to use such activities. A fifth area, keeping students accountable for work, is presented in Chapter 3.

As you read the items below, you can note ideas for procedures on Checklist 2 at the end of this chapter.

GENERAL PROCEDURES

Beginning-of-Period Procedures

On five or more occasions every day, you will need to begin a class period. It is important to conduct this activity efficiently so that you will be able to begin content activities quickly. The following five items cover the things most frequently involved in getting the period underway.

Attendance Check

Choose a place where your seating chart, absence slips, tardy slips, and grade book can be conveniently stored. Typically this will be in your desk or at a lectern or table at the front of the room. You should have an unobstructed view of all the students from this location. Keep a seating chart for each class period, and use this seating chart to check attendance. You may wish to call roll for the first few days of class until you get to know the students' names and then use a seating chart afterward. After you fill out the absence slip for the office, note the names of absent students in your grade book. An alternative strategy is to call roll each day from your grade book and note absent students as you call the roll.

Students Absent the Previous Day

As these students enter the room, they can leave their absence slips at the location where you check attendance. You can sign and return the absence slip while you are checking roll, immediately after, or during the first seatwork activity. To facilitate these students' getting the handouts they might have missed, use a system of writing the absent students' names and the date on each copy and put these in an absentee file. Direct returning students to the absentee folder for missed papers.

Tardy Students

Most schools have a policy in this area; if yours does, be sure to follow it consistently. Teachers who begin to deviate from tardiness policies (for example, letting students slip into the classroom if they are only a few seconds late) will soon find that the rate of student tardiness will increase and that their beginning-of-class procedures will break down. Tardiness to class can become a nagging management problem if you allow it. If there is no specific school policy or norm, you will need to develop a procedure of your own. Some teachers assign detention before or after school each time students are tardy without a valid excuse. Other teachers give a warning for the first incident and then provide detention or some other penalty beginning with the second occurrence of tardiness. You should keep a record of tardy students just as you keep a record of absences. A simple system is to mark a *t* in the grade book each time a student is tardy, just as you might record an *a* for absence. Another system is to put a spiral tablet or a clipboard on a table or attach it somewhere near the door. When the tardy students enter the room, they sign in before taking their seats. This preserves a record of tardy students and allows you to continue your instruction without interruption. You can then check tardiness permits at a convenient time.

Behavior Expected of All Students

Students should be told what they are expected to do at the beginning of the period while you are handling the administrative tasks. They should know that they are expected to be in the room (some teachers require that they also be seated at their desks) when the bell rings, or else they will be counted as tardy. Once the bell rings, socializing should stop. Good managers often handle the beginning-of-class activity in one of two ways. Students may be given a regular activity that they are expected to perform at the beginning of every period. Some teachers use a warmup in which several problems, a question, or some very brief assignment is displayed on the chalkboard or on the overhead projector screen. The question or problems may review the preceding day's assignments. An alternative to a work assignment is for the teacher to display an outline of activities for the class period. Students are expected to copy this in their notebook or on an assignment sheet. Another way to begin class is to tell students to use the time to get out any needed materials (headings on papers if needed, homework papers, textbooks, project materials, and so on) and to remain seated with no talking until you finish your administrative matters. This will work only as long as you handle these matters quickly and do not leave students in dead time for very long.

Leaving the Room

Occasionally students will need to leave your room during the period; for example, to use the bathroom, get a drink of water, take medication, or go the library, to the school office, or to another area of the building. Schools usually have policies for handling these matters, typically requiring the use of a hall pass signed by the teacher or by office personnel. Most effective managers discourage trips to the bathroom or water fountain except for emergencies. Sometimes keeping a record of requests will deter overuse. Unfortunately, liberal policies in this area frequently result in classroom (and school) management problems.

A second area that is sometimes troublesome concerns whether students are allowed to return to their lockers to retrieve materials during the class period. Frequently teachers do not allow this at all and require that the students sit in class without materials or look at another student's text. In such a case the student might receive reduced credit for work not brought to class. Other procedures that are sometimes used are to allow the student to return to the locker to obtain the necessary materials, but to impose a mild penalty or count him or her as tardy. Whatever policies you establish, the overriding considerations are to minimize the number of students who go out of the room for noninstructional purposes and to follow your procedures consistently.

Use of Materials and Equipment

Your classroom will have a variety of materials and equipment. Identify those things that you expect students to use and indicate how these items should be operated and under what conditions. This should be done as soon as students are expected to use the equipment. There may also be a number of items in the room that you do not want students to use or handle. Identify these to the students and explain your rationale for keeping these off-limits.

Equipment and Materials for Students

These items include the pencil sharpener, student desks, tables, special equipment such as microscopes, globes, encyclopedias, dictionaries, and other room materials. You will need to establish procedures for the use of whatever items you have in your room. A common procedure for the pencil sharpener is to request that students sharpen pencils before the tardy bell rings and not during activities in which the teacher is presenting or instructing the whole class. If students need to sharpen their pencils during seatwork, only one student at a time is allowed at the pencil sharpener. A variation on this common procedure is to allow two students at the sharpener—one sharpening and one waiting. Still another variation is to require two sharpened pencils at the beginning of class. If students have access to storage cabinets, bookshelves, or equipment in different parts of the room, you need to identify how and when these different areas and materials may be used.

Teacher Materials and Equipment

Included here are the teacher's desk, storage areas, filing cabinet, and closet, as well as your own personal possessions. You should make it clear to students that they are not to take things from your desk or use your supplies without permission. Older, more mature senior high students generally do not need to be told this procedure unless, of course, you observe students taking liberties with your materials. However, you should state the expectation to younger students, especially to middle school or junior high classes. Be pleasant about it when you explain it, and the rationale for the procedure is so obvious that you need not dwell on it.

Ending the Period

Just as one needs procedures to begin a period, so too are routines helpful at its close. Two items are of general concern: getting students and the room ready for the end of the period and dismissing class. Any room equipment or materials used during instructional activities must be returned to their storage spaces. Any cleanup of materials and equipment should be accomplished before the end-of-period bell. Finally, you may wish to remind students of particular items needed for the next day or for future activities. Consequently, you need to leave sufficient time at the end of the period for whatever cleanup and announcements are required. If students have been engaged in seat-work with their own materials, then only a short time (less than half a minute or so) may be needed to put materials away. You will have to judge the time needed and signal the students when to begin cleaning up. Sometimes students will stop work and get ready to go well in advance of the bell. If you tell students that you will let them know when they should begin to clean up or to put their materials away, they will be less likely to develop this habit. Be conscientious about giving students sufficient time before the bell rings. They have a limited amount of time to get to their next class, and it is not fair to them or to their next teacher to cause them to be tardy.

The second item of concern in ending the class is the signal for dismissal. Many teachers prefer to dismiss the students themselves rather than allow the end-of-period bell to be the students' signal. This allows the teacher to hold the students in their seats if the room is not yet properly cleaned up or if an announcement remains to be given. If you wish to use this procedure, you will need to tell the students that you—rather than the bell—will dismiss them and that they should remain in their seats until you give a signal indicating that it is appropriate to leave. If you use this procedure, some students are sure to test it by leaving their seats when the bell rings. In such a case you must be prepared to call them back to their seats. You might then dismiss all the students except for those who left their seats early.

PROCEDURES DURING SEATWORK AND TEACHER-LED INSTRUCTION

Good procedures for these activities are especially important because it is during these times that much instruction and learning take place. Good procedures will prevent or reduce the interruptions or distractions that can slow down content development activities or interfere with student work.

Student Attention During Presentations

It is helpful to consider how students should behave when you are presenting information to the class or while you are conducting a discussion or recitation. Students are typically expected to listen attentively to the teacher and to other students. (In fact, teachers often translate this expectation into a general classroom rule.) Teachers also expect that students should neither engage in social conversation with each other during such activities nor read unrelated materials or work on other assignments. The simplest way to enforce the latter requirement is to require that only books or other materials needed for the lesson be on the students' desks. You may also want students to take notes during your presentations. If so, you need to state explicitly that this is desired, and you will need to teach your students how to do it. Many students will be unable to abstract key points from your presentations, so you will need to help them by telling them what they should record in their notes, or by providing an outline on the chalkboard or overhead transparency. You could also provide students with a partially filled-in outline, with directions to complete it after the presentation. If note taking is expected, you should show them how you expect their notebooks to be organized. This means presenting an example of a properly organized notebook and periodically inspecting student notebooks.

Student Participation

You will need to identify some procedure by which students can ask a question, contribute to discussion, or receive help without interrupting you or other students during whole-class activities. During presentations and discussions the simplest procedure is to require that students raise their hands and wait to be called on. But do not limit class participation only to volunteers. Call on all students and be sure that everyone has a response opportunity. In most circumstances it is not a good idea to allow students to call out comments or answers without raising their hands. Undesirable consequences of allowing call-outs include domination of participation by a few students, frequent inappropriate comments, and interruptions of discussions and presentations. Teachers who rely on call-outs may get an inaccurate impression of overall understanding. Requiring that students raise their hands before commenting or asking questions gives all students an opportunity to participate. Two exceptions to the "no call-out" procedure are reasonable. The first occurs when teachers want students to provide a chorus response; that is, a whole-class response to a question. This can be handled by telling students at the beginning of the activity that they do not need to raise their hands. Also, many teachers use a nonverbal signal for a chorus response—such as cupping one hand behind an ear—or a verbal signal—such as prefacing the question with a cue word such as, "Everyone, . . . " A second exception may occur during activities in which hand raising might slow down or interfere with a class discussion. Again, students can be told that it is not necessary to raise hands during that particular activity.

It is worth noting that such variations from a standard procedure generally should not be used early in the school year. Instead, follow a simple routine for several weeks until you are certain that students understand it. Then, if you choose to depart from the procedure, clearly communicate the difference to the students at the beginning of the activity.

Procedures for Seatwork

In many subject areas students are frequently given assignments to work on in class. During such activities the teacher usually circulates around the room monitoring students and providing individual feedback. A number of procedural areas should be planned ahead of time so that you are able to direct student efforts while they engage in this activity.

Talk among Students

Some effective managers do not allow any student talk during seatwork activities. They require that students work on their own, that they neither seek nor provide help to other students, and that they refrain from socializing. Other effective managers allow quiet talking among students when such talk is content related. You will have to decide what your policy will be. The "no talking" rule is easier to monitor, and you may want to start with this procedure during the first month or two of the school year and then try allowing students to help each other on a trial basis. If you decide to allow students to talk to one another or to work together during seat-work activities, you will need to establish specific limitations. For example, you might say that during certain activities quiet talking is allowed, but if it gets too loud, the privilege will be lost. Be specific about what you mean by "quiet talking," that is, whispering, low-volume natural talking, or talk that can be heard no more than two feet away.

Obtaining Help

When students are working at their seats and need help, you should have them raise their hands. You may then go to them or have them come to you one at a time. This procedure will avoid the formation of long lines of chatty students at your desk. It will also allow you to control where you give individual assistance. If you choose to help students at a location other than their desks, choose one that allows you an unhindered view of the rest of the class. But remember that moving among students helps keep them on task.

Out-of-Seat Procedures

To eliminate unnecessary wandering around the room during seatwork, you should indicate when students are allowed to leave their seats. For example, students may sharpen pencils, turn in papers, get supplies, and so forth, only when necessary. Trash can be kept at each student's desk and discarded at the end of the period. A one-at-a-time rule often works for movement during seatwork.

When Seatwork Has Been Completed

Sometimes one or several students will finish their seatwork before the end of the period or before the next scheduled activity. This circumstance is frequently handled either by having students complete an additional, enrichment assignment for extra credit, or by allowing such students to use the remaining time for free reading or to work on assignments from other classes. If you have enrichment activities that involve additional materials not in the students' possession, you will need to specify when these materials may be used, where they will be kept, and what the procedures are for returning the materials to their proper place. Note that if many students frequently complete their work early, this is evidence of insufficient assignments or spending too much time in seatwork activities rather than content development.

PROCEDURES FOR STUDENT GROUP WORK

Sometimes an assignment or activity will require that students work together in groups. Examples include some laboratory assignments in science classes, the preparation of group reports or projects in social studies and English, homemaking labs, or study groups organized to accomplish specific learning objectives or to prepare for an exam. When small group work is taking place, the teacher usually monitors the whole class and responds to requests for help from groups. A number of procedures to help small group activities proceed smoothly are described below and also in Chapter 5.

Use of Materials and Supplies

Small-group activities, particularly those that are run as part of a laboratory, frequently require the use of a variety of materials and equipment. To avoid traffic jams you must plan distribution stations carefully and use more than one if necessary. When possible, save time by placing some or all needed materials on students' desks or worktables before class starts. Be sure to check equipment for proper functioning ahead of time and have replacements on hand for use when needed. Student helpers may be assigned to distribute supplies and materials, to monitor supply stations, and to clean up work areas. If students need to bring special materials for group or project work, they should be told far enough in advance so that they can obtain them, and you may have to locate safe places for materials to be stored while work is in progress. If any of the equipment poses a potential hazard to students or can be easily damaged by careless use, you will need to identify safety routines and plan appropriate demonstrations.

Assignment of Students to Groups

This will be important for several reasons. First, students who do not work well together should probably not be placed in the same work group. Also, a group composed mainly of poorly motivated students is not likely to accomplish much. One strategy is to try to have at least two capable students assigned to each group and to spread the less-able or less-motivated students across all the groups. If each person's grade is then based partly upon the individual's accomplishments and partly upon the group's accomplishments, everyone in the group has a stake in what everyone else does, and the chances for a successful experience are increased. To obtain groups that are well balanced for ability, to discourage social talk during the assignment, and to save time in forming groups and getting started on the task, assignment of individual students to groups should be determined ahead of time by the teacher.

Student Goals and Participation

Students need to be told specifically what they are supposed to accomplish in their small group work and taught how to go about the task. It is a good idea to assign specific roles and to discuss with students ahead of time the different roles they will take in the group work (e.g., reader, recorder, reporter, etc.). Preparing a list of steps that should be followed and displaying it on a chalkboard, on an overhead projector transparency, or on a handout can help the students monitor their own progress. You might even suggest time allotments for accomplishing each step.

Other areas of behavior such as out-of-seat movement, contacting the teacher, and so on, can be managed using the same procedures as have been identified for seatwork activities. Obviously, quiet talk should be permitted, but the noise level may become a problem. Impress students with the importance of keeping talk task focused. During the activity monitor the groups carefully and stop inappropriate behavior quickly at the individual or group level before it spreads to the whole class. You may want to identify a signal you will use to warn the class if the noise level gets too high.

Learning Teams

An instructional method that makes extensive use of groups is called learning teams or cooperative learning groups. This method has been applied widely in many subjects and grade levels. Typical practices are for teams to be formed heterogeneously and to work on academic tasks requiring interdependent action. Evaluation criteria reward the group for individual achievement, thus encouraging cooperation; teams may compete against each other and be rewarded on the basis of group performance. Procedures for learning teams incorporate many of the factors described in the preceding sections on the use of small groups, but they also have some unique characteristics. Therefore if you plan to use them, be sure to study the method further; some good sources are books by Slavin, Sharan, Kagan, Hertz-Lazarowitz, Webb, and Schmuck (1985) and Johnson and Johnson (1975).

MISCELLANEOUS PROCEDURES

A few other procedures merit mention. Although not all of these will be of concern to you, some may be helpful to consider.

Signals

A signal is some action, behavior, or physical prop that is used to obtain student attention or to indicate that some procedure or behavior is called for. If you always begin instruction by moving to a specific location in the room where you stand facing students, they will learn that you are giving them a signal that instruction is about to begin. Some teachers like to have a readily identifiable signal to notify students that seatwork or group work activity is about to end and that another activity will soon begin. Examples of such signals include turning the lights off momentarily, ringing a bell, or turning on the overhead projector. Any signals that you intend to use should be explained to the students. The class should not have to guess what you are trying to accomplish.

Public Address (PA) Announcements and Other Interruptions

It is important that you and your students be able to hear PA announcements. Therefore, you should explain that during such announcements there is to be no talking and students should not attempt to ask you questions or leave their desks. You should also listen during these announcements. This shows respect for your own rules. Other interruptions such as visitors, office workers seeking information or forms, loud noises in the hall, and so forth may be a frequent distraction in your school. You can reduce their effects by teaching your students a procedure to handle interruptions. A simple one is to indicate that whenever you are interrupted, students should either sit quietly with no talking if they have no assignment, read a book, or continue working if they already have an assignment. Be sure to have at least one set of handouts ready, in case the interruption is very long.

Special Equipment and Materials

If you have special equipment or materials that are likely to capture students' immediate interest (for example a minicomputer or live animals), decide on policies for access and use, and communicate them to students right away. For most special equipment, learning centers, and special materials, however, wait until the first time they are actually to be used to give a demonstration and instructions. You can also make a list of specific instructions and post it where the materials or equipment will be used.

Fire and Disaster Drills

Find out what procedures are used in your building. Because most secondary students know the basic procedures, a few timely sentences during the first week about the procedure for leaving the room (for example, by row) and where to go will be sufficient. You may want to post a map of where students are supposed to go. Eventually a schoolwide rehearsal will be held.

Split Lunch Period

Tell students whether they should clear their desks or leave their work out when they are dismissed for lunch. Tell them if it is safe to leave personal belongings in the room. Show or tell the class what route they should take from your room to the cafeteria and remind them of school areas that are off-limits and of proper hallway behavior. Be specific as to what time class will resume and stick to it; otherwise, you will find students wasting five or more minutes every day.

SUGGESTED ACTIVITIES

1. Identify the schoolwide rules and procedures you and your students are expected to observe. Be sure these are incorporated into your own classroom rules and procedures where appropriate.

2. Read Case Studies 2-1 and 2-2 on the following pages. They illustrate classroom procedures and rules for most major areas, and they will be helpful as you develop your own system of management.

3. Use Checklist 2 at the end of the chapter to help organize your planning of classroom procedures. Be sure you think through your expectations for student behavior in each of the general areas as well as in instructional areas that you will be using. Then develop a set of procedures that will communicate your expectations to your students.

4. If you have trouble developing procedures in some area or are not sure that the ones you have selected will work, be sure to check them out with other, more experienced teachers. They will usually be more than happy to share some of their "tricks of the trade."

5. Develop a list of four to eight general classroom rules. Be sure they emphasize areas of classroom behavior that are important to you and to the functioning of your classroom.

6. After you have developed a set of rules, review them with an administrator or with another teacher in your subject area. If you do not know whom to choose, ask several teachers or a counselor for nominations.

CASE STUDY 2-1

RULES AND PROCEDURES IN AN EIGHTH-GRADE CLASS

The classroom rules in Ms. Ashley's English class were simple: Be prompt, be prepared, be polite, and be quiet. When the tardy bell rang each day, students were expected to be in their seats copying the plan of the day from the overhead transparency. This plan usually included the topic, objectives, and materials for the day's lesson and the assignment for homework. Thus, the beginning class routine consisted of putting away their books, getting out their spiral notebooks, recording the date, and copying a daily plan. While the students did this, the teacher checked roll. If students were tardy to class, they immediately signed a tardy roster on a table by the door and took their seats. The penalty for unexcused tardiness was thirty minutes of detention after school. Students who had a valid excuse checked the "Please excuse" column on the tardy roster and left their "tardy excuse form" in a tray next to the roster.

The rule "Be prepared" required that students bring their materials and completed homework assignments to class each day. Students were not allowed to return to their lockers. Late papers were not accepted, but incomplete work was accepted for partial credit.

The rule "Be polite" required that students not interrupt the teacher or other students when they were speaking to the class. To avoid interruptions and to give everyone an opportunity to speak during whole-class discussions or instruction, students were required to raise their hands to get permission to speak. But the teacher did not limit questioning only to volunteers; any student could be called on at any time. This rule also covered listening carefully when the teacher or another student was addressing the class. Students were not to use the pencil sharpener or do other distracting things during these times. Students were to treat other students with consideration.

Students in Ms. Ashley's class were expected to use quiet voices during activities in which talking was permitted. These included small group or class discussion activities or when the teacher had given special permission. Students were not allowed to talk among themselves during individual seatwork activities.

Ms. Ashley's students were allowed to leave their seats to turn in work at designated trays or get supplies of materials from shelves without permission from the teacher, but if individuals wandered and bothered other students, they lost their privilege and had to raise their hands for permission. When seatwork began, the teacher circulated among students, checked progress, and gave individual feedback and/or instruction. She later sat at a worktable from which she could easily watch students while she helped individuals or small groups.

Students raised their hands for permission to come to the table. Sometimes the table was used for peer tutoring, which the teacher arranged.

Consequences of breaking class rules or not following procedures were related to a schoolwide system of demerits. Demerits resulted in detention after school and in contacting parents. Ms. Ashley emphasized communication with parents about student behavior and work. She called students' parents with good news as well as bad, and each grading term she presented awards to two groups of students: those with very good attendance and behavior records and those who did outstanding work or improved their work during the term.

Each day Ms. Ashley used the last few minutes of class for cleanup and announcements. If students were working on seatwork, she had them stop, get their supplies ready to go, return materials to shelves, and check around their desks for papers and trash. Then she made announcements of upcoming events and reminded students of any unusual supplies they would need to bring the following day. After the bell rang she dismissed her students.

 ## CASE STUDY 2-2

PROCEDURES FOR SMALL-GROUP WORK/LABORATORY ACTIVITIES

The day before her science class had its first laboratory assignment, Ms. Davis discussed procedures and rules for group work and use of the laboratory facilities. The rules and procedures she discussed included the following guidelines:

1. Work with your assigned partner(s). Participate, do your share of the work, and be polite and considerate.

2. Raise your hand for assistance from the teacher. Don't call out.

3. All talk should be quiet and work related.

4. Stay at your group work stations unless it is necessary to get supplies. Don't wander or return to your desk until the teacher tells you to.

5. Read instructions on the board, overhead transparency, and worksheet, and listen to the teacher's instructions.

6. When you finish work, check over your worksheet to be sure it is complete and neat. If there is extra time, ask the teacher for more lab instructions. If there are none, read the references listed for the day's lesson.

7. The teacher dismisses the class. The class will not be dismissed until the laboratory area is clean.

8. Report broken equipment quietly and quickly to the teacher.

9. Obey laboratory safety rules: Never turn on gas jets unless instructed; never put anything in electrical outlets; never drink from laboratory faucets; stay out of the laboratory storeroom; keep your hands away from your mouth and eyes; wash your hands after laboratory activities; no horseplay.

Students in this class worked in pairs for most laboratory activities. Partner assignments were changed several times during the year, not at every lab session. On the day of a lab, the teacher began activities by quickly going over the objectives of the lesson, the grading criteria, and the procedures listed on the lab worksheet. If the laboratory activities consisted of several major parts, the teacher suggested time allotments for each part to help students pace themselves. The teacher also had a list of some references in the text and readings from other sources in the room for students to read for background when completing the worksheet, studying for a quiz, or as an enrichment activity in case a student completed all assigned work early. New words or terms used on the worksheet were defined. All this information was already listed on the blackboard or on an overhead transparency to save time. If the laboratory work involved many procedures, the teacher helped students divide up the work. For example, jobs for Partner A and for Partner B were listed separately either on the chalkboard or overhead. Two separate supply stations were often used to avoid congestion.

During lab activities the teacher circulated and answered questions of students who raised their hands. The teacher gave several reminders about time, providing a ten-minute, a five-minute, and a two-minute warning before cleanup. She allowed plenty of time for cleanup (usually at least five minutes before the end of the period). To make sure the class did not run overtime, she used a kitchen timer. Immediately after cleanup, the teacher had all students return to their desks. There she gave them a quick report on their behavior during the lab and also on any common procedural or academic problems. This information was helpful to students in future lab sessions and in filling out or correcting their worksheet for the day.

Sometimes this teacher used work groups for discussions, problem-solving sessions, or test review. For these activities the teacher decided on group assignments ahead of time and listed names of students in each group on an overhead transparency. On the transparency she would also indicate specific responsibilities within groups (for example, discussion leader, recorder, reporter, supplier). Tables and/or groups of desks were numbered before students arrived, and students were told to sit in the group indicated on the overhead transparency. In arranging seating beforehand, the teacher spread these groups as far apart as possible in the classroom. Then, as soon as class began, the teacher went over the objectives, procedures, and grading criteria for the activity before letting students begin work. To structure the groups' activities, the teacher provided a worksheet to guide students. As in laboratory activities; the teacher suggested time allotments, and she often used a kitchen timer to help her. Especially at the beginning of the year, the teacher reminded students of the classroom rules for group work. As students worked in groups, she carried a clipboard so that she could easily record participation grades. At the end of group discussion activities, students always filled out self-evaluations on how well their group had met the objectives of the lesson, on how well they had followed the small group activity rules, and on how well they, individually, had met their responsibilities to their group.

 ## CHECKLIST 2

RULES AND PROCEDURES

Check When Complete	Area	What Is Your Procedure in This Area?
	General Procedures	
☐	A. Beginning-of-period	_____
	1. Attendance check	_____
	2. Previously absent students	_____
	3. Tardy students	_____
	4. Expected student behavior	_____
☐	B. Out-of-room policies	_____
☐	C. Materials and equipment	_____
	1. What to bring to class	_____
	2. Pencil sharpener	_____
	3. Other room equipment	_____
	4. Student contact with teacher's desk, storage, other materials	_____
☐	D. Ending the period	_____
	Seatwork and Instruction Procedures	
☐	A. Student attention	_____
☐	B. Student participation	_____

Check When Complete		Area	What Is Your Procedure in This Area?
☐	C.	Seatwork procedures	_____
		1. Talk among students	_____
		2. Obtaining help	_____
		3. Out-of-seat	_____
		4. When seatwork has been completed	_____
	Student Group Work		
☐	A.	Use of materials and supplies	_____
☐	B.	Assignment of students to groups	_____
☐	C.	Student participation and behavior	_____
	Miscellaneous		
☐	A.	Behavior during interruptions	_____
☐	B.	Special equipment	_____
☐	C.	Fire and disaster drills	_____
☐	D.	Split lunch period	_____
☐	E.	Lockers	_____

3

Managing
Student Work

When we presented a set of procedures for establishing an orderly classroom setting in Chapter 2, we also indicated that additional procedures would be needed to help manage student work. In this chapter we will describe the additional procedures, which are aimed at encouraging students to complete assignments and to engage in other learning activities.

In all of the academic core subjects and in many of the others, students are given assignments or projects frequently, perhaps even daily. Projects, written assignments, problem sets, and a variety of other academic tasks are typical of the secondary school curriculum. Sometimes these assignments are to be done in class; at other times they are given as homework, or perhaps both. These assignments are important for learning and retention because they provide systematic practice, application, and repeated exposure to concepts. Consequently, consistent and accurate completion of academic work is a critical goal for effective management. However, when procedures for managing student work are not working well or when students are not held accountable for their performance, then many problems can occur. Consider the following example:

> Toward the end of the first grading period, Ms. Peters noticed several disturbing signs of lack of student interest in completing written work in her social studies classes. The deadline had passed for students to turn in their first major project of the year, a report on their state's water resources, and fewer than half the students had met the deadline. Ms. Peters then extended the due date by one week. But even with the extension, one quarter of the reports were not turned in. Those reports that were completed were disappointing, because many consisted mainly of pictures of water scenes clipped from magazines and a short discussion taken from an encyclopedia reference that Ms. Peters had suggested as one resource—not as the sole source of information. Many of the reports looked as though they had been thrown together the night before they were due. With a sinking feeling Ms. Peters realized that if she graded strictly, many students would do poorly. Because she had intended to use the report for a major portion of the grade, many students were in danger of failing. To make matters worse, numerous students had not been completing recent shorter assignments, and many of those that were completed were of poor quality. These had not been demanding assignments and they were well within most students' capabilities. The activities included completing worksheets and answering questions listed at the end of the text chapters. Ms. Peters typically had students do two or three of these assignments each week and place them in their notebooks. She collected them every three weeks and assigned a grade to the notebook. Of the students who did complete all assignments, quite a few did them poorly, with very sloppy or partially completed work. Again Ms. Peters felt herself caught in a dilemma. If she graded strictly (or just fairly), many students would fail, and she might face great resistance from both students and their parents. However, if she relaxed her grading standards, students would learn that they could get away with not doing their work.

It is safe to say that many students in Ms. Peters's classes do not feel accountable for completing work carefully or on time. The basis for the lack of student cooperation could be determined from answers to the following questions:

- Do students know how each assignment contributes to their overall grade?

- Are requirements for assignments clear with respect to standards for quality, amount of work, and due dates?

- Is student progress being monitored frequently?

■ What kinds of feedback do students receive about their progress as well as about their completed work? How immediate is the feedback?

These questions suggest important areas of accountability. In each area Ms. Peters could have done several things to encourage students to complete assignments promptly and correctly. This chapter will focus on aspects of classroom procedures that communicate the importance of work assignments, enable students to understand what is expected of them, and help them make desired progress. Critical procedures for which you must plan include your grading system, monitoring and feedback, and communicating assignments and work requirements. Each of these areas is discussed below. Checklist 3 is provided to help organize your planning in these areas. In addition, some case studies are provided at the end of the chapter.

YOUR GRADING SYSTEM

At the end of each grading period, you will need to record a report card grade for each student. How you determine this grade has important implications for classroom management. Grades are very important to most students (and to their parents) because they are tangible evidence of student accomplishment. It is therefore important that your grading system accurately reflect the quality of student work. In addition, you will want to use your grading system to help ensure that students complete their assignments by the due dates.

The first thing you should do before deciding on a grading system is to determine whether your department, school, or district has any policies that you must follow. Usually a school or district will have established a numerical standard for grades (for example, 90–100 = A, 80–89 = B, and so on). If so, you will need to become familiar with the policy and adapt your grading system to it.

After determining the relevant school policies, you should identify the components of your grading system. Remember that the most accurate assessment of performance generally will be based on frequent evaluation of all aspects of student work, not just on a few test scores or a major project grade. A system that incorporates a daily grade that contributes significantly to an overall grade allows for frequent evaluation and feedback and keeps students accountable for their everyday work; it is an important aid to the academic success of many students. In subjects which have individual projects extending over several days or weeks (for example, industrial arts, home economics, or writing projects in English), a teacher can still examine student work daily and record a grade, or note "satisfactory" or "not satisfactory" progress. In addition to daily assignments, other frequently used components of grading systems are tests, papers, projects, workbooks, quizzes, performance, quality of participation (as in discussions), and extra-credit work. Many teachers include student notebook grades in their grading system. Students are required to keep all their work organized in a notebook, which is graded periodically for completeness and neatness. Often students must make corrections on all graded work before putting it in their notebooks. If you want students to keep notebooks, you should be explicit about what should be placed in the notebook and how it should be organized. It would be a good idea to include this information in a course syllabus. In addition, the notebook should include a table of contents and/or a list of assignments. Also, a sample notebook can be displayed so that students can see what is required. These practices encourage students to be organized and help them keep track of materials they need to study for exams. In planning your grading system, be sure that you can manage the bookkeeping aspects, and remember that you will have to evaluate twenty-five to thirty or more students in each class.

After you have identified the components of your grading system, decide what percentage of a student's grade each component will represent. Once you have established your system for grading, you might wish to prepare a handout for students explaining the basis for grading and describing the major components. You can have them take this home to be signed by a parent. This procedure has several virtues. For one thing, it makes very clear to the students what criteria will be used to determine the grade. It also informs the parents, who may then be of some assistance in monitoring progress or assisting their child, Having sent this information to the parents, you may find it helpful later in the year to refer to it when discussing their child's progress in your class.

You will also need to set up your grade book so that important information can be entered into it. You will find it most convenient if you record all relevant information for each student in the grade book rather than keeping separate lists of student numbers and book numbers, absences, project grades, and so on. Leave an extra line between student names in order to provide space for the additional information. You can use the top line for each student to record a daily grade or homework score and to note absences or tardiness (write an "a" or "t") in the upper right-hand corner of the space, using pencil in case the absent student arrives late). Use the other spaces to record any other information (for example, quiz or project grades) that might be collected on the same day. Some teachers like to use pens of different colors to highlight different components of their grading system. Using more than one line per student might require that you use a second page for a larger class, and thus you might run out of pages before the year is over. Get a second grading book if you need to. Finally, to enable you to turn quickly to the appropriate page, place small index clips (paper clips will do, if necessary) or color-coded plastic tabs on the appropriate page for each class.

Reprinted by permission of King Features Syndicate.

FEEDBACK AND MONITORING PROCEDURES

In conjunction with a system for recording and assigning grades, you should have other procedures for giving students feedback about their performance. Regular feedback is more desirable than sporadic feedback because it offers students more information and reduces the amount of time they practice making errors if their performance is incorrect. If you give daily assignments, you will almost certainly wish to involve students in checking them, because your time will be too limited to check 125 to 150 assignments every day. Of course, you cannot expect students to check complex assignments calling for advanced levels of knowledge (for example, essay scoring). However, many daily assignments are of a more routine nature and can be checked by students. The following procedures will be helpful to keep in mind:

1. Students can be allowed to check some of their own assignments. You can reduce the temptation to be dishonest by requiring that a different color pen (or pencil) be used for checking. When students do check and correct their own work, you need to monitor them closely and then collect and spot-check the papers yourself.

2. You can also have students exchange papers for checking. Establish a routine for this to save time; have the papers passed in the same way each day. Vary the pattern every few weeks to avoid "too friendly" grading.

3. Describe and model to students how you want the checking done; for example, mark or circle incorrect answers, put "graded by" and their name in a specified place on the paper, put the number missed or correct or the grade at the top of the first page, and so on.

4. You can record grades by having students call them out, or you can collect the papers and record the grades later. If students call out their grades,

you should still collect the papers occasionally and examine them. Hold students responsible for accurate checking. If a student feels that his or her paper was marked incorrectly by another student, a simple system is to have the student write a note to that effect on a designated part of the paper. You can then verify the work when you examine the papers.

Another type of feedback includes having students keep their own record of daily grades, quizzes, and so on. Some teachers have students calculate a weekly or biweekly average from this record during a few minutes of class time. This type of self-monitoring keeps students informed about how they are progressing and makes obvious the effects of failure to turn in assignments.

When you have students working on long-term projects, it is important to help them make satisfactory progress. Break the assignment into smaller parts or checkpoints and then set deadlines and goals for each part. A term paper, for example, might have intermediate checkpoints established for (1) a description of the topic and thesis statement, (2) a list of sources and an outline, and (3) a rough draft. It is not necessary (or efficient) to collect the interim products; instead, circulate around the room to check each student's work and give feedback. You might assign a letter grade for satisfactory progress at some major checkpoint, though most teachers who use checkpoints use a simpler "satisfactory/unsatisfactory" assessment. For a construction project a plan or description of the project or major stages in its completion can be evaluated as an intermediate check.

Monitoring Student Work in Progress

Once you have made an assignment, you should give careful attention to student work. Group seatwork needs a guided beginning. If you immediately begin work at your desk or go to help one student without first checking to see that all are working, some students may not even begin and others may proceed incorrectly. Two simple strategies will help avoid this situation. First, you can assure a smooth transition into seatwork by beginning it as a whole-class activity; that is, have everyone take out papers, worksheets, or other materials, and then answer the first question or two or work the first few problems together as a group, just as you would conduct a recitation. For example, ask the first question, solicit an answer, discuss it, and have students record it on their papers. Not only will this procedure ensure that all students begin working, but immediate problems with the assignment can be solved. A second way to monitor student involvement in the assignment is to circulate around the room and check each student's progress periodically. This allows corrective feedback to be given when needed and helps keep students responsible for appropriate progress. Avoid going only to students who raise their hands seeking assistance, or else you will never note the progress of other students who may be unwilling to ask for help.

Reprinted by permission: Tribune Media Services.

Long-Range Monitoring

Be sure to use your grade-book records to monitor completion rates and performance levels on assignments. The first time a student fails to turn in an assignment, talk with him or her about it. If the student needs help, give help, but require that the work be done. If the student neglects two assignments consecutively or begins a pattern of skipping occasional assignments, call the parent(s) or send a note home immediately. Be friendly and encouraging, but insist that the work be done. Don't delay making contacts with the home, and above all don't rely on using just the grade at the end of the grading period to communicate that a student's performance is below par. By then a pattern of poor performance may have developed, and both you and the student will find it difficult to recoup.

COMMUNICATING ASSIGNMENTS AND WORK REQUIREMENTS

Student accountability will be greater when students have a clear idea of what their assignments are and what is expected of them. This means that the teacher must be able to explain all requirements and features of the assignments. However, that alone will not be enough: Not all students will listen carefully, some students may be absent when the assignment and requirements are discussed, and the assignment itself may be very complex. In addition, there is more to completing assignments than doing the work accurately—you must also consider standards for neatness, legibility, and form. While we do not want to encourage an overemphasis on form to the detriment of the content objectives, some standards in these areas need to be set. After all, good work habits, neatness, and careful attention to detail are valued attributes in most occupations. The following three areas should be considered.

Instructions for Assignments

In addition to an oral explanation of the assignment requirements, you should post the assignment and important instructions on a chalkboard in a place marked "Do not erase." Use the routine of requiring that students copy the assignment into a notebook or onto an assignment sheet. It is a good idea to record each day's assignment for a whole week (or more) somewhere in the classroom. This is helpful to students who have been absent.

The grading criteria and requirements for each assignment should be clear. Be sure you explain these to the students. If the instructions are complex, as for a long-term project, it is best to duplicate the instructions and requirements or have students copy the instructions into their notebooks. If in-class performance is to be evaluated, as in a home economics class or science lab, tell students exactly what you will be rating (for example, following correct laboratory procedures, working quietly and cooperatively, cleaning up) and how much weight (or how many points) each factor will carry. Be realistic in your grading criteria and systematic in following through with your evaluation.

Standards for Form, Neatness, and Due Dates

You'll need to decide whether students may use pencil or pen and what color or colors of ink are acceptable. Also, you need to decide and communicate to students what type of paper and notebook are to be used in class and whether students should write on the backs of pages. A policy for neatness should also be determined. Students need to know whether you will accept paper torn from a spiral notebook, how to treat errors (for example, draw a line through them, circle them, erase), and how stringent you are about legibility. You should also think about the consequences for students in this area if they do not do work properly. For example, will you deduct points or reduce the grade on the assignment? Because some students may turn in incomplete work, you need to decide whether you will accept it and grade only what is done, subtracting the part not done from the grade, or if you will accept papers only when complete.

Decide on a heading for students to use on their papers. Post a sample heading, have students make copies to keep in their notebooks, and go over it with students the first time they are to use it. Remind them of this heading several times during the early weeks of school, and tell them the consequences of neglecting to use the proper heading (for example, five points deducted from grade).

Finally, due dates must be reasonable and clear; exceptions should not be made without good cause. Classwork should be turned in before students leave class. Accept late homework only with a written excuse from parents, or impose a penalty such as reduction in grade. The reason underlying this firmness is that many secondary students still require active help to avoid procrastination.

Procedures for Absent Students

When students are absent from classes, they miss instruction, directions for assignments, and assistance they may need in getting work underway. Establishing routines for handling makeup work can be very helpful to returning students. Routines will also help prevent these students from milling around your desk asking questions about missed assignments and from interrupting you to obtain directions for makeup work. The following items should be considered:

1. As mentioned earlier, post weekly assignment lists on a bulletin board or keep a folder with lists of assignments in an accessible place so that absent students can determine what work they missed without interrupting you. Keep an "absentee" folder for each class and place in it copies of handouts students miss.

2. Decide how much time is allowed for making up work, and stick to it.

3. Set up a place where students can turn in makeup work and where they can pick it up after it has been checked (for example, baskets or trays labeled "Absent In" and "Absent Out"). The "Absent Out" basket will also provide a place where students can pick up any graded work that was distributed while they were absent.

4. Establish a regular time, such as fifteen minutes before or after school, when you will be available to assist students with makeup work. Also, you can designate class helpers who will be available at particular times of the class period (usually during seatwork) to help students with makeup work.

SUGGESTED ACTIVITIES

1. Use Checklist 3 at the end of the chapter to organize your plan for managing student work. Note areas where you are not certain of your procedures and then seek advice. You should also read the case studies at the end of this chapter for additional ideas.

2. Reread the case study used to introduce this chapter. Suggest some procedures or actions this teacher might have taken to prevent the problems she is facing.

3. Read Case Studies 3-1, 3-2, and 3-3, noting positive examples and ideas you might apply to your own classroom. Then read Case Study 3-4 and suggest ways the teacher might revise her procedures to manage her class better.

CASE STUDY 3-1

AN ACCOUNTABILITY SYSTEM IN AN ENGLISH CLASS

Ms. Clark posted a weekly chart listing daily activities and showing maximum number of points students could earn for each activity (a possible 100 points for daily work and tests per week). In addition, the students kept a copy of the weekly chart in their notebooks, recorded the points they earned beside each assignment, and had the sheet signed by their parents each week. Also on the chart was a list of books and materials to bring to class each day.

In addition to the weekly chart, the teacher listed daily activities in detail on the front chalkboard. Her lessons followed the order on the list, and several times during each class period she pointed out to students their progress on the list. When describing seatwork assignments, she told students how much time they would have to complete each assignment; she then actively monitored students as they worked, circulating and providing assistance. During class discussions she made sure that all students participated by calling on nonvolunteers as well as volunteers at least once and by keeping a checklist to be sure everyone responded.

Students who had been absent were responsible for finding their assignments on the weekly list, conferring with the teacher before or after school, and filing makeup work in a special folder when completed. Students picked up papers that were handed back in their absence from an "absent basket." The first few times the teacher placed an absent student's paper into this basket, she reminded the class whose responsibility it was to get the paper.

Ms. Clark was consistent in her procedures for checking student work. She had students check their own work with red pen or pencil, or she had students trade papers to check. She always collected papers afterward. Sometimes she had students turn papers in for checking and grading. Students recorded their points on their weekly assignment sheets when the papers were handed back. All papers for the week were handed back by the end of class on Friday. Students were expected to record their grades on their assignment sheets and have their parents sign them by Tuesday of the next week.

CASE STUDY 3-2

MANAGING STUDENT WORK IN A MATH CLASS

An important tool in Mr. Richard's accountability system was a notebook he required that his students maintain. On the first day of class, he introduced it by showing a sample notebook. In addition to daily assignments and tests, the notebook included a grade sheet which was sectioned for recording homework grades, test grades, pop quiz scores, and a notebook score. Students recorded their grades on this page each marking period, calculated an average, and compared their computations with the teacher's to verify their grades. Major tests were put in the notebooks after having been signed by parents. The notebook also had a section for the class notes which students regularly took during presentations. Mr. Richard collected and assigned a grade to student notebooks a week before the end of the grading period. The notebook grade was given a weight equal to a major test grade in determining the student's course grade. Although he did not collect the notebooks until late in the grading period, Mr. Richard circulated around the room to check notebooks several times before collecting them. The first time he checked the notebooks, shortly after the beginning of the first grading period, Mr. Richard simply looked for correct form and made sure that each student had begun using a notebook. Several weeks later he would check to be certain that the students were including the appropriate material and continuing to follow correct procedures.

Each day's assignment was written on the front board. Beginning on the fourth day of school, students did warmup problems immediately upon entering the room. These problems were displayed on the overhead projector screen, and students were to hand in their work when the teacher finished checking roll. These daily exercises were always graded and returned to the students either at the end of the period or on the following day.

Homework was always checked and had to be completed on time. Mr. Richard explained to the students that it would not be fair to those who completed their homework promptly for others to have more time or perhaps the opportunity to copy answers from another student's completed paper. When students were taught how to average their grades, Mr. Richard also demonstrated the effect a zero would have on their homework average.

When students returned to class with a homework assignment, they were given explicit instructions on how to exchange their papers and how to mark them. Mr. Richard told them to listen carefully to his instructions for exchanging papers, as he would have them do it differently on some days. One example was, "If I say, 'Pass it forward,' you pass it to the person in front of you. Then those of you in the front of each row should walk quietly to the end of the row and give your paper to that student." When work was checked by students, Mr. Richard frequently asked who had missed a particular problem. If many students had difficulty, he explained the problem to them in detail. After the papers were checked, he told students how to determine the grade. Points were deducted if a student failed to use pencil or did not write out each problem. He then told students to pass the papers back to their owners.

Mr. Richard usually called on students for their grades and recorded them in his grade book. If students thought their papers had been graded incorrectly, they were to tell him the grade they were given and put the paper in a designated place on his desk so that he could check it at a later time. At least once a week, Mr. Richard collected students' homework papers and checked them himself. After recording grades during class, or when he returned papers to students, he reminded them to record their grades on their grade sheet in their notebook.

 CASE STUDY 3-3

MANAGING LONG-TERM ASSIGNMENTS

In Ms. Curry's science class students completed two research papers during the year. Ms. Curry had carefully planned the procedures to help students be successful on these assignments. For the first research paper, she assigned topics rather than allowing students to choose their own. An assigned topic made it easier for students to begin quickly and allowed the teacher to make some adjustments in the difficulty of the assignment for different ability levels of students. When she introduced the first research paper, Ms. Curry gave her students two handouts describing requirements. On one page was a description of the topic for the paper and some questions that it should cover. The other handout was the same for all students. This outlined general requirements for the research paper, a calendar of checkpoints and a due date for the assignment, and information about how the research paper would be graded. Ms. Curry went over all the directions and requirements with the students. One requirement was neatness. These standards were defined in detail and included information about acceptable color of ink, final appearance of the paper, the type of folder to be used for the report, and procedures for corrections. Another requirement concerned references and the bibliography. Students were to use at least three references and a standard form for compiling the bibliography. There was a specific requirement for the number of written or typed pages of text. The teacher provided examples of research papers from prior years for students to examine during class. She also indicated the days the class would be scheduled to work in the library. The checkpoints for the project included an initial approval of the list of references identified by each student. Ms. Curry also examined the students' notes. At both these checkpoints she gave students feedback about the appropriateness of their sources or work. Ms. Curry gave two grades, one based on the written report and the second based on the students' oral report to the class. Before the written report was due, students received a check-off sheet that they could use to determine whether they had met all the requirements before turning in their reports. Before the oral reports were given, Ms. Curry gave students copies of the checksheet she used for evaluating and recording grades for each presentation. She discussed with students each item on the evaluation checksheet.

CASE STUDY 3-4

POOR WORK AND STUDY HABITS IN MATHEMATICS

Ms. Wood's mathematics classes are free of serious disruptions, and for the most part, students pay attention to her presentations. In her first-year and second-year algebra classes, in which most of the students are very conscious of report card grades and seem serious about doing well in school, conduct problems are limited to isolated cases. In the three sections of general mathematics that Ms. Wood teaches, students are less task oriented and more inclined to misbehave. Nonetheless, students usually observe major class rules and procedures, with most of the inappropriate behavior being limited to off-task socializing or inattentiveness.

Ms. Wood's classes are not without problems, however; numerous students are falling behind in their work and are receiving low grades as a result of their poor performance on chapter tests. These tests are used as 75 percent of the report card grade, with the remaining 25 percent based on a score assigned to each student's notebook, which is turned in at the end of the grading period. At the beginning of the year, students were told to keep all classwork and homework assignments in the notebook along with any daily notes they might take. Their notebook grade is based on an overall score assigned by the teacher one week before the end of the grading period. "After you check each assignment in class, be certain to place it in the notebook so that it will be there when I determine notebook grades," Ms. Wood told her students. "Otherwise, you will not receive credit for doing your assignments." About once a week Ms. Wood collects daily work and checks it herself; however, numerous students do not turn in completed homework assignments. The students in the algebra classes have followed the instructions for notebooks reasonably well, although several in each class have presented incomplete notebooks at grading time. In the general math classes, more of the student notebooks are poorly done, with many assignments missing and contents sloppily assembled. A handful of students in each class have not bothered to turn in notebooks at all. Ms. Wood found herself getting annoyed a few days before the notebooks were due, when many students asked what was supposed to be in them. As a result of the confusion over the contents, Ms. Wood allowed an extra several days for students to turn in the notebooks, and she told students to listen more carefully the next time she explained a course requirement.

During presentations to classes Ms. Wood holds students' attention well because she presents new concepts and procedures clearly. She always explains each type of problem that students are likely to encounter, and she demonstrates solutions and a rationale using several examples. Ms. Wood generally works at her desk while students do seatwork, although she allows them to come up to her desk for assistance when they encounter difficulty or when they need to determine what work they have missed while they were absent. As the year has progressed, Ms. Wood has observed more and more students doing poorly on their exams, presenting incomplete or sloppy notebooks, and receiving low grades.

CHECKLIST 3

ACCOUNTABILITY PROCEDURES

Check When Complete		Area	Notes
	Grading System		
☐	A.	Does your school have a policy in this area?	_____
☐	B.	What components will your grading system have?	_____
☐	C.	Weight or percent for each component?	_____
☐	D.	How will you organize your grade book?	_____
	Feedback and Monitoring		
☐	A.	What checking procedures will you use?	_____
☐	B.	What records of their work will students keep?	_____
☐	C.	When and how will you monitor classwork?	_____
☐	D.	When and how will you monitor projects or longer assignments?	_____
	Communicating Assignments		
☐	A.	How will assignments be posted or otherwise communicated?	_____
☐	B.	What grading criteria and other requirements will be described?	_____

Check When Complete		Area	Notes

☐	C.	What standards for form and neatness will you have?
		    pencil, color of pen
		    type of paper
		    incomplete work
		    late work
		    heading	

☐	D.	What procedures will you establish for makeup work?
		    assignment list
		    handouts
		    time for completion
		    where to turn in
		    help for absentees	

4 Getting Off to a Good Start

The first few weeks of school are especially important for classroom management because during this time your students will learn behaviors and procedures needed throughout the year. Your major goal for the beginning of the year is to obtain student cooperation in two key areas: following your rules and procedures and successfully completing all work assignments. Attaining this goal will establish a classroom climate that supports learning, and it will help your students acquire good work habits and attitudes toward your subject.

Getting off to a good start requires careful attention to how you will teach your rules and procedures to your classes, introduce your course to the students, plan lessons and assignments, and decide on the sequence and amounts of time for various activities. This chapter will address these topics and consider some special problems encountered during the first week or so of classes. In addition, three case studies of beginning-of-year activities in secondary school classrooms are presented along with a checklist that will help organize your planning for the first weeks of school.

PERSPECTIVES ON THE BEGINNING OF THE YEAR

Several principles described below should guide your planning for the beginning-of-year classroom activities.

1. **Resolve student uncertainties.** When your students arrive on the first day, they will not be sure of your expectations for behavior or of your course requirements. Although previous experiences in other teachers' classrooms will have given them general expectations about what constitutes acceptable or unacceptable behaviors in school, they will not know what you expect in your classroom. For example, should they raise their hands if they want to comment or ask a question? May they leave their seats without permission? May they speak to each other during seatwork or at other times? Moreover, the students do not know how consistently you will enforce your procedures and rules or what the consequences will be if they do not follow them. In addition, they will be unfamiliar with your system for grading and other accountability procedures. Because of these uncertainties, you will be in a very good position at the beginning of the year to help students learn appropriate behavior by providing a specific, concrete description of your expectations for behavior, course requirements, and standards for work. However, if you do not take advantage of this opportunity, students may begin to behave in ways that interfere with good instruction and learning. You will then face the more difficult task of eliminating unacceptable behavior and substituting more appropriate behavior in its place.

   Take the necessary time during the first few days of classes to describe carefully your expectations for behavior and work. Do not be in such a hurry to get started on content activities that you neglect to teach good behavior. Rather, combine learning about procedures, rules, and course requirements with your initial content activities in order to build the foundation for the whole semester's or year's program.

2. **Help students be successful by planning uncomplicated lessons.** Your content activities and assignments during the first week should be selected and designed to ensure maximum success by students; students should feel secure and optimistic about their ability to do well in your class.

3. **Keep a whole-class focus.** When planning activities for the first week, you should maintain a whole-class focus. Presentations and discussions should be made to all the students at the same time and not to parts of the

"Good morning class. My name is Miss Applegate.
One false move and I'll kill you."

© Leo Cullum

class in small groups. Seatwork assignments should be the same for everyone, although you can have extra-credit, enrichment assignments available to challenge the students who complete seatwork assignments early. Restricting the type of activity will keep your classroom procedures simple and avoid activities that might make it difficult for you to monitor students or prevent inappropriate behavior. After your classes are running smoothly and students have learned correct behavior, you can use more complex activities, if they are appropriate.

4. **Be available, visible, and in charge.** You must stay in charge of all the students all the time. Be where you can see what they are doing; do not get so involved working with one or a few students that you lose contact with the remainder of the class. Stay away from your desk unless absolutely necessary and move around during seatwork to check on student progress. Doing these things will keep students more involved, and you will be available to assist students when needed.

PLANNING FOR A GOOD BEGINNING

Before you plan classroom activities for the first week, you need to have your room and materials ready and to have identified your rules, procedures, and consequences. If you have used the checklists and suggestions in Chapters 1 through 3, you are ready to consider a few final items.

Procedures for Obtaining Books and Checking Them out to Students

Be sure you know what procedures to use to obtain books and have on hand any needed forms to record book numbers and names of students. If there is no special form, you can record book numbers in your grade book. Some teachers prefer not to enter student names into their grade book until sections have been leveled and enrollment stabilizes. If you choose to wait, you can record book numbers on the class roster sheet instead of the grade book and transfer them to the grade book later.

Procedures for Checking out Textbooks

Be sure to wait until students have been assigned their lockers before you check out textbooks. Then have a supply of book covers on hand so that students can cover their books promptly. Many teachers check out textbooks by the second or third day of classes and do so during a content activity. A common procedure is to distribute the textbooks to students at the beginning of the activity, indicating whether the books need to be covered and any other relevant information, such as the cost of the book if lost. Later, after students have begun the seatwork portion of the lesson, they can be called to the teacher's desk one or two at a time so that the teacher can record their book numbers and note any damage to used books.

Required Paper Work

Have all forms on hand. Use file folders for each class period to keep these materials separate and organized.

Class Rosters

Be sure you have these organized by period. Note any special students who have handicapping conditions that must be taken into account in seating or who require medication. You will probably be told whether you have any such students by a special education teacher or counselor. These professionals are also a useful source of suggestions for working with such students in your classes.

Another way to keep records until classes stabilize is to use a set of 3-by-5 cards for each class. Have one card for each student and record on it the student's name, book number, and attendance and grades for the first two weeks. This not only makes it easier to move student records from period to period as schedules are finalized, but it also provides a set of name cards for use throughout the year to make sure all students are called on. Some teachers have students write their own names, parents' names, telephone numbers, and other useful information on these cards.

Seating Assignments

Plan to assign seats during the first week of classes. Assigned desks allow you to make a seating chart from which you can learn student names and also check attendance quickly. There is little point in assigning seats on the first day of classes unless you are quite sure that very few changes in your class rosters will occur. By the second or third day, however, class rolls may stabilize enough for permanent seating.

Some differences in seating assignment practices are observed in junior and senior high schools. It is more common at the junior high school level for teachers to assign seats, often alphabetically. (An advantage of alphabetical seating is that assignments can be collected in the same order that you will record them in your grade book, thus saving you some time. Multiplied by five classes, the gain in efficiency is significant.) At the senior high level some teachers assign seats, while other teachers allow students to choose their seats. In the latter case the chosen seat is the permanent one; that is, students are not allowed to move around at will. Also, teachers reserve the right to reassign students to different seats if necessary. Whatever the grade level, you can change seating arrangements later in the year to accommodate work groups, to move students who need close supervision to more accessible seats, or just to provide a change.

First-Week Bell Schedule

Find out how much time is available for each period during the first week. Some class periods may be shortened to accommodate extra long advisory or homeroom periods. If so, find out which periods are affected and how much time will be available for each class.

Tardiness during the First Days of Classes

Most teachers do not attempt to enforce their tardiness policies during the first two days of classes—students are still trying to find classrooms, and the time for passing between periods is not always predictable. By the third class day, however, it is usually reasonable to expect all students to arrive at your classroom on time. Tell them the day before that you will begin to count students tardy unless they are in your room before the bell begins to ring (or whatever your policy is). Then enforce the policy the next day and thereafter.

Administrative Tasks

If you have not already done so as part of Chapter 2 activities, be sure you know what special administrative tasks are required during the first week. If you have a homeroom or advisory class, be sure to keep its forms and materials in separate file folders.

Rules

You will discuss your expectations for behavior with your students on the first day you meet with them and as many times thereafter as needed. You can list rules on a large chart and post it on a bulletin board or a wall. You can also distribute copies of rules or display them on the chalkboard or overhead projector screen and have students copy them into their notebooks. If you have not yet decided on classroom rules, you should review the relevant section in Chapter 2.

Course Requirements

You will need to discuss course requirements with your students during the first week. You should outline the major requirements such as tests, pop quizzes, a notebook, projects, and homework, indicating how they contribute to the students' grades. You do not need to list each requirement in great detail, but you should indicate the major features. It is a good practice to provide students with a copy of your requirements—perhaps on the same sheet as your classroom rules. Some teachers have students take it home for parents to sign.

A Beginning-of-Class Routine

Decide what standard routine you will use to open each period. The routine should enable students to make the transition into your classroom in an orderly manner, ready for instruction. It also will allow you to check attendance and perform other administrative tasks quickly and without interruption. If you have not yet decided on a beginning-of-period routine, you should review the relevant section in Chapter 2. Whatever your opening routine, students should complete it without talking, remaining seated and quiet until you are ready to begin instruction.

Time Fillers

You should prepare constructive academic activities for occasions when extra minutes are available and students have nothing to do. This is especially likely to occur during the first week or two of classes, when the bell schedule may be altered unexpectedly. Examples of time fillers include worksheets, puzzles, and logic problems related to your subject. You may find books containing such fillers among the supplementary materials in your department's storeroom, in a book store, or in a teachers' supply store. You may also order them from teachers' supply catalogs. Further, you should check the teachers' edition of your textbook for ideas. Frequently a section of enrichment or supplemental exercises, questions, or problems can be used either as a seatwork assignment or as a whole-class recitation topic. You might also allow individuals who complete work early to have free reading time while they are waiting for the next activity to begin. You might keep a shelf of books and magazines for such times. Content-related materials are, of course, the most desirable items for such reading.

ACTIVITIES ON THE FIRST DAY OF CLASSES

For class periods of normal or nearly normal length, your first-day activities will generally include administrative tasks, introducing your course to students, communicating your course requirements and expectations for student conduct, and an initial content activity. For shortened class periods some of the discussion of course requirements can be postponed, and the content activity can be shortened or eliminated. First-day activities are described below in a commonly used sequence. Where significant variations in the activity or sequence may occur, they are noted in the discussion.

Before and at the Bell

Before the bell rings stand near the door or immediately outside the door. Help students find the correct room, and prevent groups of students from congregating nearby and blocking your doorway. Students will have an easier time finding your room if you post a sign with your name outside the door. Usually students enter quickly and quietly on the first day; however, should some students enter in an unacceptable manner, you can have them repeat their entrance properly or tell them that they are expected to enter quietly and without commotion in the future.

Greet students pleasantly, but do not start long conversations. Tell students that they may choose their seats for the day, and when most students have arrived, you should enter the room. When in the room, help students be seated, stay in prominent view, and monitor student behavior. When the bell rings, tell students your name and the course title (this information should also be listed on the chalkboard), and ask students to check their schedules to be sure they are in the correct room.

Administrative Tasks

Have all necessary materials close at hand so that you can begin quickly. You will first need to check attendance. When you do, have students raise their hands (rather than call out) when you call their names so that you can begin to associate names with faces. Using this procedure conveys the idea that hand raising is more desirable than call-outs. Pronunciations and preferred names can be noted on the class roster at this time. If students must complete forms or class cards, or if you must take care of other administrative matters at this time, tell students what needs to be done and what behavior is expected of them; for example, "After you fill in the class cards, hold them at your seat until I call for them to be passed in." To facilitate the completion of class cards or other forms, write the needed information on the chalkboard or display it on the overhead projector.

Introductions

Tell students your name and something about yourself, such as your interests, hobbies, family, or why you enjoy teaching your subject. If many students do not know each other, you can use a brief get-acquainted activity. You can also have students complete a short questionnaire identifying interests, hobbies, or experiences related to your subject. Afterward, give students an introduction to your course, including an overview of topics to be covered. Try to emphasize the course's importance, interest, challenge, and applications. Mention some activities that will be of interest to the students, so that they can begin the year looking forward to taking the course.

Discussion of Class Rules

During this activity you will discuss your expectations for student conduct. Refer to the rules (some teachers prefer to call them "Guidelines") you have posted, displayed on the overhead projector, or made available on a handout. Read each rule and explain it, giving examples when needed. Describe the rationale for each rule and any penalties associated with breaking it. You can involve students in this discussion by asking them for examples or reasons for particular rules. Because students are often reserved in their class behavior on the first day or two of school, don't expect eager participation in this discussion. If you intend to use special incentives you could also introduce them now, or you might save this discussion for later in the week. If your rules do not already incorporate major procedures, you should discuss your expectations in these areas at this time. Students should understand what is acceptable with respect to student talk, how to contact the teacher for help, when movement about the room is permitted, and how to ask questions or volunteer an answer or comment. In addition, your procedures for tardy students and beginning the period should be explained. Do not go over procedures that will not be needed soon; you can discuss them when they are needed. Unless particular school rules are relevant for your classroom, you do not need to include these in your discussion; they probably will be discussed by a building administrator on the public address system or in a general assembly, or teachers may cover them during a homeroom or advisory period. Of course, if such a presentation has not occurred, you should go over the rules briefly during your first-period class for the benefit of students who are new to the building.

Some senior high teachers, particularly in the upper grades, prefer a less explicit approach to class rules. They do not identify expectations as "rules," nor do they post or otherwise provide copies of rules. They limit their discussions of expectations for conduct to a few major areas, such as tardiness and student talk. However, this does not mean that such teachers have no expectations in other areas of behavior—they are quick to give feedback when students' behavior is not acceptable. For example, if such a teacher is presenting material to the class, and students leave their seats, the teacher will use the incident to tell the class that students should remain in their seats during presentations. The advantage of this approach is that it invites cooperation by recognizing that many older senior high students are well acquainted with prevailing school norms and will behave acceptably with no prompting. The disadvantage of this approach is that it places a considerable burden on the teacher's ability to monitor students' behavior so that initial deviations from expectations can be detected. If they are not detected, students may believe that the behavior is acceptable; consequently, more inappropriate behavior may occur. Note that the less explicit approach to rules is the practice of only some senior high teachers. Other good managers at this level are more systematic in their presentation of expectations for student conduct. Finally, we note that the less explicit approach should not be used at the junior high level or for ninth graders; these students benefit from the structure provided by an explicit set of rules and expectations for major procedures.

When you present and discuss your rules and procedures with the students you should set a positive tone, emphasizing the benefits to all: "These rules are intended to help us have a class atmosphere that is appropriate for learning. We all know that a classroom will work better when everyone respects other's rights." Or, "An orderly class helps everyone by giving students a good chance to listen and learn and to do their work without being bothered or interfered with."

If some procedure or rule will be difficult to follow, you might acknowledge the students' feelings as you discuss it: "I know it isn't easy to remember to raise your hands before speaking during a discussion, but doing so will give everyone a chance to participate," or "It will be hard not to start using the new equipment right away, but we need to wait for directions so no one is injured." Such expressions of empathy when presenting rules that may appear arbitrary have been found to help students later exhibit more self-control.

Presentation of Course Requirements

Describe briefly the major course requirements and indicate how these will contribute to the course grade. It is not necessary to go into great detail about grading procedures or other course requirements unless some aspect of them will be used immediately. For example, you do not need to go over test or homework procedures at this time, but you should list on the board or display on the overhead projector screen those materials that students will need to bring to class each day. If you plan to give students a handout listing rules and major procedures, you can also include on it a list of materials and major course requirements.

When periods have been shortened, or in order to conserve time for a content activity, you may limit discussion of course requirements to the absolute essentials and wait until later in the week to fill out the picture.

An Initial Content Activity

Choose an activity that students can complete successfully with little or no assistance. This will leave you free to handle other matters and to monitor students. The activity should be an interesting one that will involve your students. Look in the teachers' edition of your textbook for ideas. Some possibilities include a review worksheet based on content from earlier grades, a subject-related puzzle, or a worksheet activity. You could also conduct a short demonstration or present an experiment, essay, story, description of an event, and so on, which you might then use as the basis for a short discussion. This could be followed by questions for which the students would write answers. Available time is a critical factor, so use an activity that can be continued the next day if the period ends before the activity. It is probably best to collect unfinished classwork at the end of the activity rather than to assign it as homework on the first day. You can then return it to students to be finished on the second day rather than relying on students to return it themselves—they may not yet have lockers, and some students will probably not have notebooks or other containers for papers on the first day.

Use the initial content activity for teaching important procedures. Begin the activity by stating what procedures students should follow. For example, if the activity is a presentation or a discussion, let students know what to do if they want to speak; for a seatwork assignment inform students how to contact you to get help.

When you introduce a procedure for the first time, follow these steps: Explain the procedure by telling the students exactly what they are expected to do; use the overhead projector or chalkboard to list the steps in the procedure if it is complex and demonstrate the procedure whenever possible; then, the first time students are expected to use the procedure, watch them carefully and give corrective feedback about their performance. For example, you will probably have students use a specific heading on written assignments. To teach this procedure introduce it when the first assignment is given. Put a sample heading on the board, go over its parts, and then have students head their own papers. You could either check the students' headings at that time or wait until you circulate around the room after the seatwork assignment has been given.

Do not use small groups, projects, individualized instruction, or any other format that requires complicated procedures, extensive student movement, or materials that students may not have with them and that you cannot supply. Help your students learn whole-class and seatwork procedures before you try more complex activities.

Ending the Period

You should establish a routine for the end of the period that helps your students get ready to leave the room as they found it and in an orderly manner. Make every effort to dismiss the class promptly to enable them to be on time to the next class. Shortly before the dismissal bell (the amount of time depends on how much cleanup needs to be done), signal your students that it is time to clean around their desks and put their materials away. If you consistently give students ample warning, you can prevent their stopping work too early.

Some teachers prefer to dismiss the students themselves, so they tell students, "Please do not leave your seats when the bell rings because I may have an announcement to make, or I may need to give you materials before you leave the class. I will tell you when you can leave the room." Such a procedure allows the teacher to wrap up any unfinished business at the end of the period as well as to hold students until they have properly cleaned up the room. Some students will almost always challenge this procedure by getting out of their seats as soon as the bell rings, so be prepared to call them back and have them wait.

THE SECOND DAY OF CLASSES

If your first day's class periods are very short, you may not be able to do much more than introduce yourself and your course and present rules and procedures. If so, you should begin the second day with a review of major class procedures and follow the first day's plan, beginning with a discussion of course requirements.

If your first day's class periods are of normal or nearly normal length, the following outline of activities may be followed on the second class day:

1. **Identify new students and get them seated.** Have them fill out class cards or any other forms from the first day. If these forms are time consuming to complete or require extensive directions, you can wait until the rest of the students are engaged in a seatwork activity before having the new students complete them.

2. **Restate the beginning-of-class routine and use it to start the period.** Perform your administrative chores, such as attendance check, at this time.

3. **Review your major rules and procedures.** Provide new students with a copy of the rules and procedures.

4. **If you did not discuss course requirements on the first day, do so now.** If students will keep a notebook or folder for your class, this is a good time to go over its organization and contents.

5. **Present a content activity.** Many teachers distribute textbooks, conduct a lesson, and then give a seatwork assignment from the text. If for some reason students cannot be assigned textbooks at this time, you can still distribute the textbooks and collect them at the end of the period. Alternatives are to provide lesson materials, such as worksheets, or to give students a pretest or some assessment of readiness for the first unit of the course. This is an especially good idea if you have not previously taught the subject, the grade level, or students with backgrounds similar to those of students in your classes.

6. **Close the period.** Use the procedure you introduced the first day.

AFTER THE SECOND DAY

Continue using the procedures you introduced on the first two days, adding new procedures as needed. Monitor student behavior carefully. Review your procedures and give students feedback when their behavior does not meet your expectations. By the third or fourth class day, you should be giving regular assignments to be done in class and at home. Check work promptly and begin using your grading procedures at once so that students receive feedback about their work and are held accountable for it.

SUGGESTED ACTIVITIES

1. Use Checklist 4 at the end of the chapter to be sure you have planned all aspects of the beginning of the year.

2. Read the Case Studies 4-1, 4-2, and 4-3. They illustrate the beginning-of-year activities in three effective managers' classes. Use these cases to help plan your own lessons for the first few days of school.

3. Read Case Study 4-4 and suggest some strategies for improving the situation.

CASE STUDY 4-1

BEGINNING THE YEAR IN A SEVENTH-GRADE MATH CLASS

First-Day Activities

Activity	Description
Greeting students	Before the bell Ms. Hunter stands just inside the doorway so that she can monitor the immediate hall area while making frequent eye contact with students as they find seats and settle in her class. Ms. Hunter smiles and greets students pleasantly as they enter the room.
Introduction (2 minutes)	When the bell sounds, Ms. Hunter goes to the center front and starts class immediately by briefly giving some information about herself: where she grew up, how long she has been teaching, how many children she has. She also announces the course title and grade level and asks students to check their schedule cards to be sure they are in the correct room.
Administrative tasks (10 minutes)	She calls roll, checking with individuals about correct pronunciation of their names. Then she passes 3-by-5 cards to the front of each row. Students take one and pass

(Continued)

Activity	Description
	others back. She explains what to put on the card: phone number, address, birthdate, and class schedule. A sample card is displayed on an overhead transparency. While students work, Ms. Hunter monitors, answers questions, and distributes a list of supplies and a sheet of class rules and procedures.
Presentation of rules and course requirements (25 minutes)	When students have finished with their cards, Ms. Hunter tells them to place the cards in the upper right-hand corner of their desks. She then begins to explain procedures and rules for this class. She shows and discusses a notebook they will be expected to keep, and she gives some information about how she will grade the notebooks. Then she discusses procedures and requirements that are listed on the sheet handed out earlier, explaining the rationale for various items and answering questions about them. Class rules are posted on a display near the door. Ms. Hunter reads them to the class and has students copy them down. She walks up and down the aisles, watching students as they write, and picking up the index cards.
Content activity (9 minutes)	The teacher assigns a math problem, written on a side chalkboard, for students to do in class. The assignment consists of a puzzle that requires computing several sums and differences that all the youngsters should be able to do. Ms. Hunter tells them that this assignment will be the first thing to go in their notebooks. Students start to work while she watches and circulates.
Closing and dismissal (4 minutes)	The teacher tells students to stop work and get ready to leave. When she asks for a show of hands of students who have finished the problem, only seven raise their hands. She announces that the problem will be on the board on the following day also, and students will be able to finish then. She calls for the papers to be passed in from the back to the front of each row and then to be held there until she collects them. With about two minutes remaining in the period, all the papers have been collected, and students have their own materials ready to go. Then Ms. Hunter asks everyone to pay careful

Activity	Description
	attention as she explains the beginning-of-class routine they will use tomorrow and every day in this class. She tells students that when they enter, they should immediately get out paper and pencil and copy and solve the review problems that are shown on the overhead screen. She will check roll while they work. The problems will be checked in class and turned in for a daily grade. She answers questions until the bell rings and then dismisses the class.

Second-Day Activities

Activity	Description
Before the bell	Ms. Hunter greets students as they enter the room and reminds them of the beginning-of-class routine she explained the day before.
Beginning-of-period routine and warmups (5 minutes)	Students take seats and get to work on multiplication problems shown on the overhead screen. As soon as the bell rings, the teacher calls roll, talks briefly to a tardy student, and gives a new student a card to fill out.
Checking (4 minutes)	Students trade papers. The teacher leads them in checking their work, calling on different students to give the answers. She uses her set of cards to call on various students and to learn names. Students pass graded warmup papers to the front of the rows, where the teacher collects them for recording.
Administrative tasks (3 minutes)	Ms. Hunter announces that she will assign seats in alphabetical order for the first term. Row by row, she calls students' names, and they move quietly to their new seats.
Presenting procedures (12 minutes)	Ms. Hunter passes out dittoed grading sheets that she and the students will use in computing their grades every six weeks. Using an example on an overhead transparency, she goes over the grade-averaging procedures to be used and demonstrates the importance of doing homework assignments.

(Continued)

Activity	Description
Content activity and administrative task (27 minutes)	Ms. Hunter distributes a worksheet for students to do in class while she checks out textbooks. The worksheet is a simple one which students can do without assistance after the teacher has demonstrated the first problem. The task includes adding numbers, determining whether the sum is even or odd, and shading areas of a diagram to produce a picture of the school emblem. Students work quietly on the assignment while the teacher calls them up one by one to check out a text. Students also cover their books. Some complete the puzzle from the first day of school.
Closing (3 minutes)	Three minutes before the bell, the teacher asks students to put their worksheets away. She briefly discusses the notebook they are supposed to have, showing the class some examples that students have already started. The bell rings and the teacher dismisses the class.

Third-Day Activities

Activity	Description
Before the bell	Ms. Hunter again greets students with a reminder of the beginning-of-class routine they are supposed to follow. The overhead projector is on as they enter. Students sharpen pencils and start to work. The teacher begins calling roll when the bell rings.
Beginning routine and administrative task (8 minutes)	Ms. Hunter allows students four minutes to work on the warmup problems; then she has them trade papers. She leads them in checking; then they pass the papers forward. She then explains that students will often trade papers and grade assignments in class: If she says "trade forward," each student passes the assignment up one student and those seated at the first of a row take their papers to those at the row's end; "trade backward" is the reverse. She helps one row demonstrate how to trade forward, and then monitors as all other rows follow her pattern. She next explains that when students grade each other's papers, they are always to use the same marking system: if an answer is right, do nothing; if an answer is

Activity	Description
	wrong, place an X in front of it. Ms. Hunter leads students in checking the problems and has students return papers to owners to see how they did. She explains how to pass up papers so they arrive at the front in alphabetical order and again demonstrates with one row how to do this. She then directs all students to pass papers forward, monitors, and collects papers from the front desks.
Content activity (30 minutes)	Ms. Hunter tells students to get out their notebooks or paper to take notes. She presents a review of sets. Students answer her questions and write down the definitions and concepts she tells them to write.
Seatwork (10 minutes)	Students are given a seatwork assignment on sets. Ms. Hunter explains that normally this would be their homework, but since this is their first real assignment, they will be allowed to finish it in class tomorrow so that she can help them and answer questions. Their homework for tonight is to finish putting together their notebooks. They will have a diagnostic test tomorrow. Students work on the sets assignment while Ms. Hunter monitors and answers questions. She also passes back the previous day's warmup exercises.
Closing (2 minutes)	Two minutes before the bell, the teacher tells students to put up their work and clean up. She dismisses them at the bell.

 CASE STUDY 4-2

BEGINNING THE YEAR IN A HIGH SCHOOL BIOLOGY CLASS

First-Day Activities

Activity	Description
Greeting students	As students enter the room before the bell rings, Ms. Holly greets students at the front of the room near the doorway, tells them to take a seat near the front of the room, and answers questions.

(Continued)

Activity	Description
Introductions (1 minute)	When the bell rings, the teacher moves to the front of the room and introduces herself. She tells them how to check their schedule to make sure they're in the right room. She gives her name and its spelling, announces the room number and course number, and tells students the abbreviations to look for on their card. Then she pleasantly welcomes them to her class.
Roll call (3 minutes)	Before the teacher begins to call roll, she explains to the students the procedures she wants them to use. She expects them to raise their hand when she calls their name and also to tell her the name they would like to be called. After roll call she records the names of two students not on her roll, after checking their class schedule cards.
Course overview (6 minutes)	Ms. Holly begins by giving an introduction to the course. She displays an overhead transparency that lists seven major topics that will be covered during the semester. The teacher describes each of the items on the list and mentions several of the activities and goals relating to each topic. Students listen quietly and ask a few questions when the teacher invites them to.
Presentation of classroom behavior policies and rules (12 minutes)	The teacher distributes a mimeographed sheet summarizing procedures and requirements for the class. She tells the students to put their name, the date, and the period at the top, and to keep these sheets at the front of their class folders at all times. The information sheet contains three sections. The first outlines eight areas of classroom procedures and rules. The second describes the notebook that is a major requirement for the course, and the third describes the grading system that will be used in the course. The teacher discusses each of the items in the procedures section in turn, and the students listen and follow on their sheets. In this manner the teacher covers policies for being on time to class and consequences for tardiness, the importance of daily attendance, procedures for making up work after absences, turning in classwork on time and consequences for late work, keeping all paper in the

Activity	Description
	science notebook and replacing lost papers, safety rules for laboratory activities, and routines for ending the class period and dismissal. The teacher displays the school handbook for students and tells them that they will go over the handbook in greater detail in class later during the week.
Discussion of grading and notebook requirements (10 minutes)	Ms. Holly then describes in some detail the system that she will use for determining grades in the class. One of the major requirements will be a notebook for all student work. She explains the requirements for this notebook: the type of folder, the importance of keeping papers in the proper order, the heading for papers, the table of contents, and the requirement that all papers in the notebook be completed and/or corrected before the notebook is turned in. After answering student questions about the notebook, the teacher describes the grading system. (Tests in the class count 40 percent of the grade. Daily work is also 40 percent, and the notebook is 20 percent. There will be two or three unit exams during each six-week period.) The teacher also mentions extra credit projects which can be done later in the grading period.
Filling out information cards, checking out books, and covering books (12 minutes)	After this presentation of procedures and requirements for the course, Ms. Holly asks students to fill out information cards. She shows a model card on an overhead transparency and goes over the items with students. Then she explains to them the procedure they will use for checking out books and covering them. Because students have been assigned their lockers, the teacher passes out textbooks and directs students to check through them for damage and write their names inside the front cover. The teacher has the name of the text and the information that students are supposed to write in their book displayed on the overhead transparency along with instructions for recording the number neatly on the class card, covering the book, and information about the cost of the book. The teacher passes out book covers, and students cover their books after completing their information cards.

(Continued)

Activity	Description
Discussion of textbook reading assignment (8 minutes)	Ms. Holly then asks students to look at a page in their text, and she introduces them to its format. She leads a discussion on how students can find the chapter objectives and use chapter titles and subtitles, along with the glossary and dictionary, to guide them in their reading. The teacher briefly discusses their reading assignment (written on the chalkboard).
Seatwork (5 minutes)	Ms. Holly distributes assignment sheets and gives directions for answering questions on the sheets as part of the homework assignment. This assignment is a simple introduction to using different parts of the textbook to locate information. Students begin work on their reading assignment or on their assignment while the teacher confers with one student about registration. When the bell rings signaling the end of class, the teacher reminds students of what to bring tomorrow and dismisses them.

Second-Day Activities

Activity	Description
Seatwork, roll call, and other administrative matters (6 minutes)	As soon as the tardy bell rings, Ms. Holly distributes a sheet for students to work on. This task is an extension of the students' classwork assignment from the previous day, an easy assignment in which students used the table of contents and book index to locate specific information. While students work on the assignment, the teacher calls roll and takes care of two new students.
Discussion of homework and seatwork assignments (12 minutes)	The teacher calls for the students' attention and begins asking questions from the previously assigned worksheets. Students volunteer answers, and the teacher leads a discussion. Students check their own papers during this discussion.
Presentation and discussion of textbook chapter (30 minutes)	Ms. Holly distributes a copy consisting of an outline of the chapter which students were to have read for homework. The outline gives the main points and allows students room to fill in additional information from the presentation.

Activity	Description
	The teacher also has a copy of the outline displayed on the overhead transparency. Students take notes as the teacher discusses the content.
End-of-class routine (2 minutes)	The teacher ends discussion of the first chapter and explains requirements for a short homework assignment. She then reminds the students that each day they are to get ready to leave class by checking their work area for neatness and making sure they have all their belongings and materials ready. She shows them where the homework assignment will be written each day on the front chalkboard along with the list of what they will need to bring to class the next day. Students are told to be sure to check this every day. The teacher answers several questions from students and leads an informal discussion until the bell rings. She then dismisses the class.

CASE STUDY 4-3

BEGINNING THE YEAR IN AN EIGHTH-GRADE ENGLISH CLASS

First-Day Activities

Activity	Description
Before the bell	As students enter, Mr. Franklin stands beside his door, nods and smiles briefly at incoming students, and periodically announces "Room 103, eighth-grade English, third period."
Administrative tasks (5 minutes)	As the bell rings, the teacher walks to the table at center front on which he has already set out and arranged his notes, overhead transparencies, and handouts for the period. He again announces the room number, course title, and period and asks all students to check schedule cards to be sure they are in the right place.

(Continued)

Activity	Description
	Mr. Franklin next takes roll. He instructs students to raise their hands and say "Present" as he calls each name. He checks for correct pronunciation and makes note of any preferred variations.
Personal introduction (3 minutes)	Mr. Franklin introduces himself and gives a bit of personal background: where he grew up, his educational background, and his hobbies. He explains that in addition to teaching English, he also sponsors the school newspaper and every year enjoys publishing the writing of his students.
Administrative tasks (7 minutes)	Mr. Franklin then explains to the class that today they will first complete an information card. He turns on the overhead projector and displays the form that students are to use: class period, name (last name first), birth date, address, phone number, parents' names, hobbies. As he explains the form, he distributes 3-by-5 cards. As students fill in the information, Mr. Franklin circulates among students and comments to several individuals on their legible penmanship. As students begin to finish, he instructs them to place the completed card at the top of the desk, take out pencil and paper for later note taking, and begin thinking about what things they would expect to be included in an eighth-grade English class. He continues to circulate and collects the completed cards.
Course introduction (7 minutes)	Mr. Franklin now calls on students to respond to the question on class expectations. He uses the information cards to call on individual students for response, and he places a check beside the names of those on whom he calls. After eliciting several student responses about content expected in his class (spelling, grammar, stories, etc.), Mr. Franklin also lists a few special areas of studies that students did not name (ballads, Greek roots, *Animal Farm*) and mentions some interesting or unusual aspects of each.
Presentation of rules and procedures (15 minutes)	Mr. Franklin next explains that there are certain rules and procedures students will need to know to do well in his class, and he wants students to know just what he expects of them. As they discuss these, students are to

Activity	Description
	take notes and to keep them in the front of their English notebook. They will start the notes today and complete them tomorrow. He tells students to head a sheet of notebook paper for notes on class rules and demonstrates with the overhead exactly how papers are to be headed with subject and period, specific assignment, name, and date. In the ensuing presentation and discussion of five classroom rules, Mr. Franklin displays each rule with the overhead, repeats it, allows students time to copy it, and gives several specific examples of what the desired behavior is and is not. At times he again uses the information cards to call on individual students for examples. After covering the rules, he tells students to head another sheet of paper for notes on classroom procedures, and he briefly circulates among the desks to see that students understand the prescribed heading. He then has students write out procedures for heading a paper, for coming properly prepared to class, and for being dismissed. He tells students to put away their notes and says they will add to them tomorrow.
Content activity (10 minutes)	As students put their notes away, Mr. Franklin explains that the short writing activity they will do next will help him learn more about class members and see how well they write complete sentences. To each row he distributes handouts, consisting of twenty-five incomplete sentences about the students and their opinions (items such as the following: Two words that describe me are _____ and _____ ; if I had $1,000 to spend today, I would _____ ; the best thing I have ever done is _____ ; someday I hope to be famous for _____ ; the most important thing in life is to _____ ; it really bugs me when people _____). As students write, Mr. Franklin monitors from the front of the room and completes some attendance forms. Students who finish early are asked to read over their sentences and think about what they have written.
Closing (3 minutes)	Three minutes before the bell rings Mr. Franklin reminds students of dismissal procedure. He then has students

(Continued)

Activity	Description
	pass up their papers, whether finished or not, and prepare to leave. He binds the information cards for the class with a red rubber band and drops them in a red-tabbed folder labeled "Third Period." The bell rings, and he dismisses the class.

Second-Day Activities

Activity	Description
Before the bell	Mr. Franklin stands beside his door and reminds students as they enter that they are to be seated and ready with pencils sharpened when the bell rings.
Administrative tasks (5 minutes)	As the bell rings, the teacher walks to the table (where again materials are organized and laid out) and calls roll. He adds the names of two students who were absent yesterday and instructs them to see him at the end of class for a copy of information given during the first class. He then announces that students will be seated in alphabetical order for at least the first six weeks. He asks all students to gather belongings and stand to the left of the desks. As he calls the names of students in each row, those students move and are seated.
Presentation of beginning routine (7 minutes)	Mr. Franklin explains that today students will begin a daily journal writing activity that will always be done during the first ten minutes of every class period. He explains that writing is a very important part of learning English and of expressing ideas and feelings; writing helps people think more clearly and communicate better. Mr. Franklin then describes his specific goals for journal writing and reads students an inspiring quote from Progoff's book on journal keeping. He asks students to take out several sheets of paper and pencil. As they do, he distributes to each student a three-hole-punched, red-tabbed file folder and three brads. He instructs students how to assemble the journal and write their names on the tabs, how to make a title page, what writing implements are acceptable, and how it will be graded. He explains that he will give a

Activity	Description
	journal grade that will count toward the course grade, but that it will mainly be based on completeness and whether the student makes an effort to write. "The main purpose is to get in the habit of writing often; your skills will improve with practice, I promise," he says. He explains that each day as they enter they will find the topic for the day's entry written in the corner of the assignment board (side chalkboard). Some days students will write on an assigned topic; other days they may write on an idea of their own selection. Mr. Franklin turns on the overhead projector and displays five of the open-ended sentences from yesterday's classwork. Below is written: "Select one of the sentences, complete it, and use it as the topic sentence of your paragraph." He announces that students will have the usual ten minutes, and those who finish early are to turn to the last sheet in the journal and jot down ideas and topics on which they might like to write in the future.
Content activity (10 minutes)	As students begin to write, Mr. Franklin actively monitors their work by circulating among them and checking to see that all are started. He then goes to the two new students and has each complete an information card, which he adds to his third-period file folder. He circulates among the students and comments to individuals on interesting ideas and good word choices.
Presentation and practice procedure (5 minutes)	After ten minutes the teacher tells students to stop writing. He explains that he will appoint an assistant each week to distribute journals before the tardy bell. Students should begin writing when the bell rings. He explains that if journals are collected in alphabetical order, it will be easy to distribute them quickly. He demonstrates with one row how to keep folders in order as they are passed up and has the entire class practice the procedure twice. He then demonstrates to students how to collect the stacks of journals from each front desk and keep them in alphabetical order. He replaces the stacks, assigns a student the weekly responsibility of collecting journals in order and placing them in the proper file box, and has that student do so.

(Continued)

Activity	Description
Presentation of procedures and information (10 minutes)	Mr. Franklin asks students to take out the notes they started yesterday and reviews rules and procedures covered thus far. He asks individual students to restate or explain these and uses the set of information cards to call on students not involved yesterday. He then presents the remainder of class procedures in the same way as yesterday, and students take notes. He includes information on his grading system, English notebook requirements, and the assignment board on which daily topics and supply requirements are listed in advance for each week. Students are told to place this information in the front of their English notebooks.
Testing (11 minutes)	Mr. Franklin then instructs students to head a piece of paper for a diagnostic grammar test. He reminds them of the correct heading form presented the first day and now displayed on a bulletin board. He watches as students prepare papers and he explains the purpose of the test: to determine at which level of grammar students are presently working.
Closing (2 minutes)	Two minutes before the bell Mr. Franklin again reminds students of the dismissal procedure and asks students to straighten their desks and pick up any trash. The bell rings, and he dismisses the class.

Third-Day Activities

Activity	Description
Before the bell	Mr. Franklin stands at the door greeting students. The appointed assistant distributes the journals.
Beginning routine (10 minutes)	The bell rings, the teacher enters, and all but two students are writing in their journals. He quietly reminds those two of the beginning class procedure, and they begin. Mr. Franklin checks to see that all are writing, checks the roll, and then circulates among students.

Activity	Description
Administrative tasks (2 minutes)	At the end of ten minutes, the teacher reminds students of the procedure for passing in journals. Students do this well, and the teacher praises their efforts. Mr. Franklin then asks students to take out a pen and the dictionaries that are already placed in their desks. He distributes as before a handout of vocabulary exercises.
Content activity and	Mr. Franklin introduces a content activity: completing a worksheet on word roots. He explains the objectives of the assignment and leads the students in doing several examples. After checking to be sure all students understand the assignment, he tells them that they have thirty minutes to complete it.
Administrative task (40 minutes)	The teacher also explains that the class will be completing an administrative task: checking out books. Each student will be called to the teacher's desk to pick up a grammar and a literature book and two covers. First, students are to complete their vocabulary assignment and place it face down on the desk before covering books. The teacher also has a crossword puzzle on root words for early finishers. The teacher finishes checking out books before most students have finished their assignment. He gives an eight-minute warning to workers, then circulates and answers questions. Students cover books or work on puzzles when they have turned in their papers.
Closing and dismissal (2 minutes)	When there are two minutes left in class, Mr. Franklin asks students to pass their assignment forward, using the same procedure as with the journals, and prepare to leave. Papers come forward in order to the front desk in each row. He collects the stacks of papers in order, clips them with a red clip, and places them in the third-period folder. The bell rings, and the teacher dismisses the class.

CASE STUDY 4-4

CONDUCT PROBLEMS IN A HISTORY CLASS

When the school year began, Mr. Davis told his American History classes that he had just one major rule for conduct—the Golden Rule. "If you'll treat others as you want to be treated, then we'll get along fine," he said. Then he added, "Just be sure to respect each other's rights, and that includes mine, and we'll all have a good year." Mr. Davis also told his students that he expected them to behave maturely because they were in high school and that if one of them got out of line, he would be quite willing to send that student to the school office to be dealt with by the assistant principal.

The classes did, indeed, function without major disruptions for several weeks. Gradually, however, almost imperceptibly, Mr. Davis began having difficulty getting students settled down to start the daily lesson. And once begun, presentations and class discussions seemed to be conducted with an undercurrent of noise as students whispered, joked, and socialized. Mr. Davis found himself interrupting the lessons more and more often to call for quiet or to remind students of what they were supposed to be doing. Problems were occurring in each class period but were worst in the sixth, the last period of the day. By the end of the fourth week of classes, Mr. Davis had sent two students to the office for persistent talking during class, including talking back to him when he asked them to be quiet. Sixth-period behavior was better for a day or so afterward, but students were soon back to being noisy and inattentive. The following description of the sixth-period class a few days later is typical.

At the beginning of the period, Mr. Davis had written a discussion question on the chalkboard. While he checked roll and returned papers, students were supposed to write a paragraph answering the question in preparation for a class discussion. However, only about half the class actually did the work; other students talked, several sat doing nothing, and two students were out of their seats socializing. Mr. Davis asked one student to sit down, but he didn't. When he told a particularly noisy girl to "close your mouth," she responded, "I can't." During the discussion students who were talking at the beginning of class complained that they did not understand the question. A few students raised their hands to volunteer responses during the discussion, and Mr. Davis called on them; other students called out responses, sometimes silly ones. Later Mr. Davis assigned questions for the end of the chapter, to be turned in the next day. Most students worked on this assignment in class, although some read magazines or talked instead. Three students passed magazines back and forth until Mr. Davis told them to put the magazines away. The noise level built up and ten minutes before the end of the period, most students had stopped working and were conversing.

What are some things Mr. Davis might do to establish better behavior in his classes?

CHECKLIST 4

PREPARATION FOR THE BEGINNING OF SCHOOL

Check When Complete	Item	Notes
☐	1. Are your room and materials preparation complete? (See Chapter 1.)	_____
☐	2. Have you decided on your class procedures and rules and their associated consequences? (See Chapters 2, 3, and 6.)	_____
☐	3. Are you familiar with the parts of the building to which you may send students (e.g., library, bathrooms, etc.) and do you know what procedures should be followed?	_____
☐	4. Have you decided what school policies and rules you will need to present to students?	_____
☐	5. Have you prepared a handout for students or a bulletin board display of rules, major class procedures, and course requirements?	_____
☐	6. Do you know what bell schedule will be followed during the first week?	_____
☐	7. Is your lesson plan for the first few days of school ready for each class?	_____
☐	8. Do you have complete class rosters?	_____
☐	9. Do you have adequate numbers of textbooks, desks, and other class materials?	_____
☐	10. Have you decided on the procedures you will use for checking out textbooks to students?	_____
☐	11. Have you prepared time fillers to use if the period is extended?	_____
☐	12. Do you know if any of your students have some handicapping condition that should be accommodated in your room arrangement or instruction?	_____

5 Planning and Conducting Instruction

Let's assume that your classroom is organized, you've developed and taught your rules and procedures, and you have systems in place to manage student work. Now that your students are attentive and ready to participate, what do you do? It is at this point that management and instruction meet. Well-planned lessons with a variety of appropriate activities support the positive learning environment that your carefully considered management decisions have begun to create. Interesting, well-paced lessons are a key to holding students' attention, while unimaginative or confusing lessons with limited opportunities for student participation are boring or frustrating to students, creating conditions for discipline problems to develop.

This chapter describes how to plan and conduct instruction in ways that support the kinds of learning you want for your students. Although this chapter is not intended to substitute for the study of specific methods of teaching particular subjects, some of the tasks of planning, organizing, and conducting instruction are basic to all content areas. Consequently, the ideas presented here should be helpful regardless of the secondary subject you teach. The chapter has three sections. The first part discusses planning decisions prior to instruction. The second section discusses how to implement those plans as you teach. The last section describes some common problem areas such as transitions between activities and clarity of instruction.

PLANNING CLASSROOM ACTIVITIES

The term *activity* describes organized behavior that the teacher and students engage in for a common purpose. Typical activities in secondary classes include discussions, recitations, presentations, seatwork, and checking, although this is by no means a complete list. Furthermore, activities are not always content based. For example, beginning-of-period activities may be mainly procedural.

Activities are an important aspect of instructional planning—they consume time, and time is a precious commodity. Class periods are usually about an hour in length, so activities must be limited accordingly. Thus, given certain learning objectives, you will need to identify those activities that will most likely lead to attaining the objectives within the allotted period of time.

You will engage in several levels of planning—both long range (e.g., by the year or semester) and short range (e.g., weekly and daily). Each of these levels of planning should be coordinated. Thus, you can divide the semester plan into units of instruction, and within units, into weekly and daily plans. This type of organization allows you to coordinate the daily activities to produce a cohesive course focusing on the main objectives and goals. Without a master plan, daily activities can appear unrelated to each other and to long-range objectives.

Objectives for daily lessons will help you decide what activities should be used. Two important considerations should be kept in mind: First, what skills or concepts must be learned to reach the objectives and, second, what tasks and activities will help students the most. In other words, your plans provide road maps to transform curriculum and objectives into activities, assignments, and tasks for students.

In addition to their potential for helping students reach learning objectives, activities are also selected, in part, for their potential for maintaining students' involvement throughout the period. For this reason, two or three activities— rather than just a single long one—should be planned for most class periods. Activities that provide for student participation or that provide each student with an opportunity to practice or apply lesson content are also desirable; they help students learn the content, and they promote high levels of involvement in the lesson.

Even though much of your daily planning for classes will focus on organizing activities, you should also keep in mind the broader perspective—your course as a whole. You need to know what knowledge and skills students are expected to develop and what units, topics, or textbook chapters are typically included in the course. Examine the teachers' edition of your textbook and preview each major section, noting statements of overall objectives and the scope and sequence of content. Identifying reasonable expectations for your grade level will be helpful when deciding on course objectives and adequate coverage of topics. Other useful sources of information about appropriate content and reasonable expectations for students in particular age and grade levels may be found in school district or state education agency curriculum guides, courses and books on instructional methods in your subject, and yearbooks of national teachers' organizations in your academic field. Finally, your department chairperson, your instructional coordinator or supervisor, or other teachers in your subject area can provide helpful suggestions on course scope and topical sequence.

Some subjects, such as English/language arts and home economics, require extra effort when developing an overall plan of content organization. Contents of these subjects include several discrete areas and frequently use more than one textbook. For example, junior high school English components include writing, usage and grammar, literature, and spelling. In order to cover diverse areas, it is common practice for several textbooks to be used. In such cases the teacher must determine an appropriate sequence for all components and decide how they will be merged into one course. If you teach one of these subjects, it will be particularly important for you to consult one or more of the information sources on curriculum mentioned in the preceding paragraph.

Types of Activities

Some of the most frequently used types of classroom activities are described below. You can think of them as building blocks for constructing your lessons.

Opening the Period

The chief concern in this activity is to help the students make an orderly transition into the classroom and be ready for the rest of the period, while the teacher handles administrative tasks such as the attendance check and helps previously absent students. We have described in Chapters 2 and 4 alternatives for structuring the opening, including the use of either academic warmups or an administrative routine with stated expectations for student behavior.

Checking Classwork or Homework

In this activity students check their own work. The activity is appropriate only when a judgment as to the correctness of the work can easily be made. Checking provides quick feedback to students about their work and allows the teacher to identify and discuss common errors on assignments. Careful monitoring during checking is important to prevent cheating. Some teachers discourage cheating by requiring that checking be done with a different color ink than the assignment, with a pencil if the assignment was completed with ball-point pen, or vice versa. When student checking is used frequently, you should collect and examine the students' papers, even when you record grades in class. This procedure will enable you to keep abreast of student progress and problems. Remember that you must teach students the appropriate procedures for checking (e.g., make no mark if the answer is correct; neatly mark an X before the item if it is wrong).

Recitation

This activity is a question-and-answer sequence in which the teacher asks questions, usually of a factual nature, and accepts or corrects student responses. This sequence of question/answer/evaluation is repeated frequently, with many students being asked to respond until a body of content has been covered. In effect, a recitation is a form of checking, done orally. It can be used to provide practice, quickly review content, or check student understanding of a previous lesson or assigned reading. It can also be used to review spelling words, vocabulary definitions in any subject, or other recall of facts.

When using recitation to check student understanding, it is important to distribute questions to all students, not just to the eager beavers. Develop a way to check systematically who gets a turn to answer, perhaps by using a checklist or name cards. Sometimes teachers do not allow students enough time to respond, thus reducing opportunities for students who are slow to answer. Some experts recommend a "wait time" of several seconds—e.g., three seconds—before giving a prompt or calling on another student.

Content Development

In this activity the teacher presents new information, elaborates or extends a concept or principle, conducts a demonstration, shows how to perform a skill, or describes how to solve a problem. During content development activities the teacher's questions are used to check student understanding and to maintain involvement. They also encourage students to contribute to the steps in problem solving, to apply concepts or principles, or to analyze the ideas being presented. In addition to questioning for comprehension, it is often a good idea to obtain work samples or other student demonstrations of the skills being taught during content development activities. Important skills for effective content development are described later under "Clarity."

Discussion

In most secondary school classes, discussions are conducted as teacher-led, whole-class activities. The purpose of using discussion is to encourage students to evaluate events, topics, or results; to clarify the basis for their judgments; and to become aware of other points of view. Sometimes discussions are begun with a recitation activity in which the facts of the content to be discussed are reviewed. Compared to a recitation, however, discussion questions are more likely to elicit student judgments and opinions, and teachers are less likely to evaluate the students' responses directly. Instead, students are encouraged to examine their opinions and beliefs and to understand other perspectives. Students may respond to each other rather than only to the teacher. The teacher's role then becomes one of clarifying and using student ideas rather than evaluating their correctness.

When using a discussion format, careful planning of questions is needed. Students should also be made aware of your ground rules for participation (for example, raise hands, listen carefully, respect each person's right to express himself or herself). Few secondary classes, especially at the middle or junior high level, can sustain a discussion for very long, so plan short ones (for example, ten minutes) until you have an idea of what you and your classes can handle. After students have acquired good discussion skills the length of this activity can be increased, when appropriate for your objectives.

Seatwork

In this activity, also known as classwork, students engage in assignments that provide practice or review of previously presented material. Often that portion of the seatwork assignment not completed in class becomes a homework assignment, unless the materials or resources needed to finish it are available only in the classroom. (Procedures for seatwork have been discussed in Chapter 2. Seatwork is more valuable for consolidating or applying prior learning through practice than for learning new content. For that reason and also because it is difficult to maintain student involvement for a long period of time in seatwork, we strongly urge you to avoid devoting large portions of class periods to this activity. A rule of thumb would be to devote no more time to seatwork than is allocated to content development activities. Seatwork should be actively monitored, with the teacher moving from student to student and providing both positive and corrective feedback.

Small-Group Work

In this activity two or more students work together. This activity might be used for drills on new vocabulary words or spelling, work on a laboratory activity in a science or homemaking class, reviewing for a test in any subject, problem solving, preparing group reports, or discussing an issue or specific topic in social studies. Small groups work best with secondary students when objectives are clear and when steps or procedures for achieving them are understood by the students. Careful monitoring of the small groups is also needed so that you can be sure they are on track and can provide assistance when needed.

One way to help discussion groups stay on track is to assign a specific role to each member and have each group responsible for reporting back to the class. Tasks could include a reader/monitor responsible for reading and clarifying the task to the group and rereading as necessary if the group gets off the subject, a turn maker responsible for seeing that all group members have equal input into the group discussion, a pacer responsible for managing the time so that all parts of the task are completed, a recorder responsible for taking notes, and a reporter responsible for presenting the result of the group's efforts to the class. Other types of group-based tasks, such as in science labs, might have somewhat different role assignments.

When assigning and managing group work, do not assume that your students possess the necessary skills for working together effectively. Instead, plan to teach them how to listen to others, take turns, summarize, reach consensus, etc. Such skills should be explained or demonstrated prior to beginning group activities and reviewed when necessary.

Closing

The goal of this procedural activity is to bring the period to an end in an orderly manner, with students ready to pass to the next class, leaving your room in good condition for your next period. Teachers usually give students a warning before the bell is to ring so that they have enough time to put materials away and get their own things ready. Other procedures for the closing activity were discussed in Chapter 2.

In the preceding discussion each activity was treated as a discrete event; in practice, activities are sometimes combined. Thus, a teacher may combine recitation and content development or discussion and recitation. If you find that using some combination of activities is more suitable for your lesson goals than planning separate activities, by all means pursue the lesson structure that helps accomplish your objectives more effectively.

ORGANIZING ACTIVITIES

The center stage of instruction is occupied by content development because it is a major vehicle for new learning. However, all class periods include other activities, and so one must plan an appropriate sequence. A commonly observed sequence of activities in secondary school classrooms is as follows:

1. Opening routine
2. Checking
3. Content development
4. Seatwork or discussion
5. Closing

Advantages of this sequence are that it has a minimum number of transition points, allows checking and feedback of the prior day's work, provides for the presentation of new material, and has a practice or an application period.

A disadvantage of the preceding sequence is that it does not easily allow for the presentation of different topics within the same period, and it also requires that the content be amenable to presentation and practice in two lengthy segments. A variation of the sequence that accommodates more than one type of content or more complex content is:

1. Opening
2. Checking
3. First content development activity
4. First seatwork activity
5. Checking
6. Second content development activity
7. Second seatwork activity
8. Closing

This sequence can be used when two different types of content must be taught within the same period and the teacher wants to provide a period of practice using classwork exercises following each content development activity. The sequence can also be used when a complex lesson is separated into two phases of content development, each followed by short periods of seatwork. Subdividing new content into two different parts with an intervening practice activity will help students consolidate learning from the first part before they are asked to contend with the new learning required in the second part. It also allows the teacher to check student understanding and provide prompt feedback.

Another advantage of this sequence is that student attention will usually be easier to maintain when individual activities are divided into shorter segments. A disadvantage of this sequence is that it produces more transition points and thus may be more difficult to manage. However, as long as the teacher is sensitive to the need to manage these transitions, the lesson format can be a useful one.

KOUNIN'S CONCEPTS FOR MANAGING GROUP INSTRUCTION

A central theme in managing activities well is the idea of activity flow. This means the degree to which a lesson proceeds smoothly without digressions, diversions, and interruptions. Lessons with a good flow will keep student attention and will be less likely to offer opportunities for deviance, because most of the cues for students will be directed toward behaviors appropriate for the lesson. When lesson flow is jerky, with frequent interruptions and side trips, there will be more competition for student attention from cues external to the focus of the lesson. Therefore there will be a greater tendency for students to go off-task.

A series of classroom research studies by Kounin and his colleagues (Kounin, 1970; Kounin and Gump, 1974; Kounin and Obradovic, 1968) identified several concepts that contribute to the effective management of interactive group activities like content development and recitations. In Kounin's studies, classroom lessons were videotaped and teacher behaviors were analyzed to determine which ones predicted classrooms with high amounts of student involvement and low levels of deviant behavior. The concepts that emerged from this research provide a rich source of ideas about conducting instruction, so we will take some time to present and discuss them.

Calvin and Hobbes   by Bill Watterson

Activity flow is maintained through three classes of teacher behaviors: preventing misbehavior, managing lesson movement, and maintaining group focus. Within each class of behavior there are two or three related concepts. Let us look at how each is defined and consider some examples. These concepts are summarized in Table 5-1.

Preventing Misbehavior

Classroom are complex settings. Many events can occur at the same time, and one cannot always anticipate what will occur or when. New teachers especially are at risk of focusing too closely on single events or on selected areas of the classroom, thus overlooking developing problems until they have spread or become disruptive. Understanding two of Kounin's (1970) concepts, withitness and overlapping, helps to prevent this mistake.

Withitness is the degree to which the teacher corrects misbehavior before it intensifies or spreads and also targets the correct student. A teacher who is not very "with it" will fail to stop a problem until it has escalated and then may require a major intervention to bring it to a halt, or else the teacher will fail to catch the perpetrator and instead target either the wrong student or a Johnny-come-lately to the scene of the crime. It is apparent that underlying aspects of withitness include good monitoring and prompt handling of inappropriate behavior.

Overlapping refers to how the teacher handles two or more simultaneous events: for example, a visitor comes to the door in the middle of a lesson; a student leaves his seat without permission while the teacher is leading a discussion; several students get into a squabble while the teacher is busy helping other students across the room. A teacher who has good overlapping skills will handle both events in some way, instead of dropping one to handle the other or ignoring the second event. To handle a long interruption, for example, a teacher might tell students to get out some work; after they have followed the direction the teacher might then deal with the interrupter. The squabble away from the teacher might be handled by eye contact or a brief verbal desist while the teacher stays in contact with the original group.

Notice that a teacher who is with it and exhibits good overlapping skills is able to insulate lessons from the intrusions that student misbehavior or external interruptions might cause. Furthermore, by reacting promptly to problems (but not overreacting) the teacher will often be able to use simple measures (eye contact, redirection, a quiet desist) that will not interfere with ongoing activities nor distract students very much. If a teacher is not very with it or does not overlap when needed, then lessons may be interrupted by student misbehavior and subsequently by the teacher's more visible and tardy reactions.

TABLE 5-1. How Effective Managers Maintain Activity Flow

Issue	Skills	Definition	Example
Preventing misbehavior	Withitness	General awareness of the classroom which is communicated to students; prompt and correct identification and correction of misbehavior	The teacher makes eye contact with a student who is about to "shoot a basket" with a wad of paper. The student puts the paper away. A student behind him, who has seen the interaction, decides he's not likely to get away with shooting a basket either.
	Overlapping	Attention to two or more simultaneous events	The teacher is leading a class discussion when a student comes in late. The teacher nods to him, continuing the discussion. Later, when students have begun a seatwork assignment, she checks in with him and signs his tardy slip.
Managing movement	Momentum	Keeping lessons moving briskly; planning carefully to avoid slowdowns	The teacher notices that explanation of a relatively minor concept is taking too long and distracting attention from the primary focus of the lesson. The teacher makes a mental note to go more in depth on this concept in a separate lesson the next day, and moves on.

Issue	Skills	Definition	Example
	Smoothness	Staying on-track with the lesson; avoiding digressions and divergences that can lead to confusion	While being responsive to student interests, the teacher avoids comments that tend to draw attention away from the key points of the lesson.
Maintaining group focus	Group alerting	Taking actions to engage the attention of the whole class while individuals are responding	Each student has a number that was drawn from a hat on the way into class. The teacher draws numbers and uses them to call on students during a fast-paced review.
	Encouraging accountability	Communicating to students that their participation will be observed and evaluated	At the end of a discussion and practice of a new skill, students are told to turn to a neighbor and explain the process to him or her.
	High participation formats	Using lessons that define behavior of students when they are not directly answering a teacher's question	While some students work problems at the board, students at their desk are instructed to check them by working the problems on paper.

Managing Movement

Whereas withitness and overlapping are accomplished by handling external interruptions and student intrusions into the flow of the lesson, movement management is accomplished by avoiding teacher-caused intrusions or delays. Good movement management is achieved through momentum and smoothness.

Momentum

This refers to pacing and is indicated by lessons that move along briskly. Teachers can cause slowdowns in momentum by overdwelling on individual parts of a lesson, direction, or skill and by unnecessarily breaking an activity into too many parts. For example, students should be taught a standard heading for assignments so it can be used routinely, rather than altering its form so that it must be explained over and over.

Smoothness

A lesson that exhibits continuity, rather than jerkiness, epitomizes this concept. A smoothly flowing lesson keeps student attention, while one that is jerky will be distracting. Kounin used graphic labels to depict ways that a teacher might diverge from a smooth lesson. He described these divergences as "dangles," "flip-flops," "thrusts," and "stimulus-boundedness." These problems are described and compared in Table 5-2.

Maintaining Group Focus

Classroom instruction involves teaching students in groups, usually a whole class at a time. Doing so means that a teacher needs to be conscious of the group influence on instruction. Like a conductor leading an orchestra, the teacher must elicit the performance of individuals and still provide signals and directions that keep the whole class together. Group focus can be maintained through several techniques.

Group Alerting

This means taking some action to engage the attention of the whole class while individuals are responding. It can take the form of creating suspense, telling students they might be called on next, calling on them randomly, asking students not reciting to listen carefully because they might be called on to add to the answer, or by using some visual aid, display, or attention-capturing strategy. In contrast, poor group alerting would be engaging in a dialogue with one student or calling on a student before asking a question so that the rest of the class does not feel the need to pay attention to the question.

Accountability

This occurs when the teacher lets students know that their performance will be observed and evaluated in some manner. It does not require a letter grade or

TABLE 5-2 Common Problems in Maintaining Momentum and Smoothness

Problem	Definition	Example
Dangle	Teacher leaves a topic or activity "dangling" to do something else or to insert some new material.	"All right, please take out your math books. Turn to page . . . Oops, I forgot to send this form to the office. Raise your hand if you ride the bus. All right, where were we?
Flip-Flop	Like a dangle, except that the topic inserted is left over from an earlier activity.	"OK, let's leave vocabulary now. We'll pick up the discussion tomorrow. Please move your chairs into your writing groups. Take your pencils and a blank piece of paper, and that's all." (Students move into their groups and the teacher begins to give instructions for today's writing activity.) "All right now, does everyone understand what I want you to do? Oh, and did everyone remember to write down their vocabulary workbook assignment? I put it on the board, pages 235–242. Ok, go ahead and start."
Thrust	Teacher inserts some information at a point where students are involved in another activity, and it seems irrelevant to them.	Students are working quietly on a standardized test. The teacher has been circulating and offering help; otherwise, there is scarcely a sound in the room. The teacher looks up and comments quietly, "When you're done, bring your test booklets to the front table and put your answer sheets in this box." Students continue to work quietly. When they begin completing their tests, the teacher must explain to each one individually where to put the test booklet and answer sheet.

(Continued)

TABLE 5-2 *(Continued)*

Problem	Definition	Example
Stimulus-bound	Teacher is distracted by some outside stimulus and draws the class's attention to it and away from the lesson.	Students are taking turns reading their writing aloud. Each student's reading is followed by comments from the rest of the class. During one such discussion, the teacher notices a student reading a paperback. "What are you reading, Alice?" she asks. "Have you read anything else by that writer?"

a score (although it might), just communicating some degree of awareness of how individual students are performing. For example, the teacher might ask everyone who knows an answer to raise a hand and then call on one or more of those students; or the teacher could have all students write down answers, perform, or display work and then circulate to check it.

Higher Participation Formats

Lessons that cue or program the behavior of students when they are not directly involved in answering a teacher's question have a higher built-in rate of participation than do lessons that merely assume that students will sit and watch when other students respond. Higher participation formats occur when students are expected to write answers, solve problems, read along, manipulate materials, or perform some other task during instruction.

Some activities lend themselves more to one type of group focus than to another. When planning instruction it will be helpful to consider which of the three aspects to use. For example, it might be difficult to use a high participation format during a demonstration that involves expensive materials, but group alerting might be easy to incorporate in the lesson.

Kounin's concepts are a stimulating addition to our repertoire for understanding how to engage students during instruction. Not only do they help identify key aspects of effective teaching, but they can be used to diagnose instructional problems and to identify possible solutions. For example, if lessons seem to drag and student response is unenthusiastic, there may be a problem with group focus; a solution may be to work on alerting or accountability or to increase the degree of participation. Activities that take too long and that seem to get off-track constantly might have a problem in the area of movement management; perhaps the teacher should check for the incidence of slow-downs and jerkiness.

TROUBLESHOOTING COMMON PROBLEMS IN CONDUCTING INSTRUCTION

The areas of transitions and clarity often cause problems during instruction. This section outlines some of the problems and suggests possible solutions.

Transitions

The interval between any two activities is a transition. In addition, the beginning and ending of periods are transitions. Several management problems can occur at these times, such as long delays before starting the next activity or high levels of inappropriate or disruptive student behavior. Some of the causes of transition problems include a lack of readiness by the teacher or the students for the next activity, unclear student expectations about appropriate behavior during transitions, and faulty procedures. Efficient transitions are important for several reasons. Much time can be wasted during poor transitions, and misbehavior can spill over into subsequent activities. Examples of transition problems are listed below along with some suggested ways of correcting these problems.

Transition Problem	Suggested Solution
Students talk loudly at the beginning of the period. The teacher is interrupted while checking attendance, and the start of content activities is delayed.	Establish a beginning-of-period routine with clear expectations for student behavior. Have a content activity ready for students to begin at once.
Students socialize too much during transitions, especially after a seatwork assignment has been given, but before they've begun working on it. Many students do not start their seatwork activity for several minutes.	Be sure students know what the assignment is; post it where they can see it easily. Work as a whole class on the first several seatwork exercises so that all students begin the lesson successfully and at the same time. Then walk around the room, check student's work, and give corrective and/or encouraging feedback.

Transition Problem	*Suggested Solution*
Students stop working well before the end-of-period bell; they then engage in excessive talking and mess up the room.	An end-of-period routine should be established: Students work until the teacher gives a signal and then they clean up around their desks before being dismissed.
Whenever the teacher attempts to move the students from one activity into another, a number of students don't make the transition but continue working on the preceding activity. This delays the start of the next activity or results in confusion.	The teacher should give the class notice a few minutes before an activity is scheduled to end. When it ends, students should be told to put all the materials from that activity away and get out any materials needed next. The teacher should monitor the transition to make sure that all students complete it; the next activity should not be started until students are ready.
A few students always seem to be slowpokes during transition, delaying the rest of the class.	Don't wait for one or two students and hold up the rest of the class. Go ahead and start, but be sure to monitor the dawdlers in later transitions in order to find out why they are having trouble. Then give them individual feedback and close supervision.
Students frequently leave their seats to socialize, come up to the teacher to ask questions, or attempt to get a bathroom permit, go to the trash basket, or wander around the room during transitions.	Define appropriate behavior during transitions and explain the rationale for limiting student behavior during these times. Monitor students and be sure procedures are established to handle out-of-seat behavior.
The teacher delays the beginning of activities to look for materials, finish attendance reporting, pass back or collect papers, or chat with individual students while the rest of the students wait.	The teacher needs to have all materials ready, and once transitions begin, the teacher should avoid doing anything that interferes with his or her ability to monitor and direct students.

Clarity

Communicating information and directions in a clear, comprehensible manner is a teaching skill of great importance. Clear instruction helps students learn faster and more successfully; it also helps students understand your directions and expectations for behavior more readily. Although clarity is important in all classroom activities, it is crucial during content development, when nearly all new subject matter is introduced and taught. Thus, this section will focus mainly on ways to improve clarity during this critical portion of the period.

Clear instruction results from several factors: the organization of information into a coherent sequence, the use of an adequate number of good illustrations or examples, precision and concreteness of expression, keeping in touch with student comprehension, and providing enough practice to ensure mastery. Some of the many ways teachers can be both clear and unclear in their instruction are described below.

Poor Clarity	Being Clear
Communicating Lesson Objectives	
Not describing the lesson's purpose or what students are expected to learn	Stating goals or major objectives at the beginning of the lesson
Pointing Out Important Information	
Not calling students' attention to main points, ideas, or concepts	Telling students what they will be accountable for knowing or doing
	Emphasizing major ideas as they are presented
	Reviewing key points or objectives at the end of the lesson
Presenting Information Systematically	
Presenting information out of sequence; skipping important points or backtracking	Outlining the lesson sequence and sticking to it
Inserting extraneous information, comments, or trivia into the lesson	Sticking to the topic; holding back on complexities until the main idea is developed
Moving from one topic to another without warning	Summarizing previous points; clearly delineating major transitions between ideas or topics

Poor Clarity	*Being Clear*
Presenting too much complex information at once or giving directions too quickly	Breaking complex content into manageable portions or steps; giving step-by-step directions, checking for understanding before proceeding

Being Specific

Presenting concepts without concrete examples	Providing a variety of concrete examples
Using overly complex vocabulary	Using words students understand; defining new vocabulary terms
Overusing negative phrases (e.g., not all insects, not many people, not very happy)	Being specific and direct (e.g., beetles, one-third of the people, enraged, discouraged)
Being ambiguous or indefinite— maybe, perhaps, sort of correct, more or less right, you know	Referring to the concrete object, stating what is and is not correct and why

Checking for Understanding

Assuming everyone understands, or simply asking, "Does everyone understand?"; then proceeding without verification	Asking questions or obtaining work samples to be *sure* students are ready to move on
Moving to the next topic because time is short or because no students ask questions	Asking students to summarize main points to verify comprehension
	Reteaching unclear parts
Not calling on slower students; relying on feedback from a few volunteers only	Systematically checking everyone's understanding

Providing for Practice and Feedback

Not assigning classwork or homework	Being sure students have adequate practice so that critical objectives are mastered

Poor Clarity	*Being Clear*
Giving assignments that cover only a portion of the learning	Reviewing assignments to be sure that all of the lesson's skills and concepts are reinforced
Not checking, reviewing, or discussing students' assigned work	Checking work regularly, reexplaining needed concepts, reteaching when appropriate

As the preceding examples illustrate, teachers can do many things to enhance (or detract from) the clarity of lessons. Following are some specific suggestions that can be applied to different aspects of your lessons and their planning.

Planning

Organize the parts of your lesson into a coherent sequence. If the lesson is complex, write down the main components. Review the unit and lesson in the teachers' edition of your textbook(s). Pay careful attention to suggestions for lesson development and activities. Study the exercises, questions, or problems provided in the textbook and decide which items would provide appropriate review of lesson objectives. Note examples, demonstrations, and key questions and activities to use in developing the main concepts. If some items in the seatwork assignment go well beyond the lesson scope, don't assign them as classwork or homework until you can teach the necessary content; or, if the content is not essential and you do not plan to teach it later, assign such items for enrichment or for extra credit.

Try to anticipate problems students may encounter in the lesson or assignments. Check for new terms and be ready to define them and present examples. Do some of the classwork or homework assignment yourself to uncover hurdles students will face. You can then build into your lesson some helpful hints or extra emphasis in these areas.

Consider the interest the lesson is likely to have for students. Will you be enthusiastic about teaching this material to your classes in this way? Your enthusiasm about the lesson is contagious and signals to students how you feel about its importance. If you find it interesting and exciting and you communicate this excitement to your class, students will probably respond with interest. If, however, you are unenthusiastic about a lesson, chances are that your students will share your feelings. Consider changing your approach in some way to put a little more spark in the activities.

Presenting New Content

If students understand where a lesson is going, they are more likely to be there with you at its end. Tell students what the lesson objectives are, either at the beginning of or during the activity. If the lesson is at all complex, give students an outline to help them follow its organization. Displaying the topical sequence helps organize the content for the students and provides a road map to keep them on course.

If students are expected to understand content from silent reading or from viewing a film or tape, provide a content outline with a few items filled in and spaces for students to supply the rest. This task focuses attention and provides motivation for careful reading or viewing.

As you present a lesson, stay with the planned sequence unless an obvious change is needed. Avoid needless digressions, interruptions, or tangential information. Inserting irrelevant information into a lesson only confuses students about what they are expected to learn. Displaying key concepts, new terms, major points, and other critical information on the overhead transparency screen or writing them on the chalkboard will underscore their importance; and, if students are required to take notes, the display will guide the information students record.

Presentation should be as focused and concrete as possible. Use examples, illustrations, demonstrations, physical props, charts, and other means of providing substance and dimension to abstractions in the lesson. Avoid the vague expressions and verbal time fillers that at best communicate little information and make presentations difficult to follow.

Checking for Understanding

Find out whether students understand a presentation during the lesson rather than later. As content development activities unfold, students can be asked questions to verify their comprehension of main points. You can also ask students to provide a written response to key questions and then check some or all of the students either orally or by examining the written work. Asking all students to

Reprinted by permission: Tribune Media Services.

demonstrate comprehension at several points during a presentation not only allows you to verify their progress, but keeps students more involved in the lesson.

Another way to check student understanding at the end of a presentation is to conduct an oral recitation on the lesson's main points. Do this by asking a series of questions that recapitulate the lesson sequence and its major concepts. Involve many students in these question-and-answer sequences so that you can identify the overall level of understanding in the class and reteach what has not been satisfactorily learned.

 ## SUGGESTED ACTIVITIES

1. Case Studies 5-1 and 5-2 describe difficulties two teachers are experiencing with organizing and presenting instruction. After reading each paragraph, review the relevant sections in this chapter and in other parts of this book and decide what strategies would be helpful in overcoming the problem. You might also use each case as a basis for a group discussion and generate a list of many possible solutions or strategies. Compare your list with that included in the key in the Appendix. Case Studies 5-3, 5-4, and 5-5 provide further opportunities for review of and practice in applying concepts from this chapter.

2. See how many examples of Kounin's concepts you can find in Case Study 5-4. Compare your list with the key in the Appendix.

3. Analyze the lesson in Case Study 5-5 by first identifying the sequence of activities used by the teacher, and then discussing what occurred within each activity. Where problems are evident, describe what alternative approaches or strategies might be used. Compare your answers with the keys in the Appendix.

 ## CASE STUDY 5-1

MS. CARPENTER

In Ms. Carpenter's class there almost always seem to be some students who don't understand presentations or assignments and who need a lot of reexplanation. While she is lecturing, students continually ask questions about what they should write in their notes. When an in-class assignment is made, Ms. Carpenter finds herself answering many questions about information just covered in the lecture. Sometimes she has to reexplain parts of the lesson to the whole class. As a result, there is often not enough time to complete activities before the end of the period. In an attempt to avoid the problems associated with note-taking, she decides to write important information on the chalkboard during the lecture. What else can Ms. Carpenter do?

CASE STUDY 5-2

MR. MILLER

Mr. Miller feels that too much time is wasted in his ninth-grade class while students get settled after class changes, get supplies ready, or move from one activity to another. While the teacher deals with students' problems, makeup work, or questions at the beginning of class, students talk and begin to play around or wander. It then takes some time to get their attention and get class started. Also, when activities change during the class period, students sometimes delay activities while they sharpen pencils or borrow supplies. Trading papers to check work in class usually results in some confusion.

Mr. Miller has already spoken with his class about the problem and has reminded them of the rules for sharpening pencils immediately upon arriving and taking seats before the bell. He tries to enforce these two rules, but he is also required to monitor the hall. What else can he do to cut down on wasted time?

CASE STUDY 5-3

MS. KENDALL

During the second week of school, Ms. Kendall is informed that too few students have signed up for her fifth-period elective humanities class. There, is, however, an overflow in fifth-period general science. Since she is certified in both English and science, the administration's solution to the enrollment problem is for her to begin Monday with the fifth-period science class. Although certified in the subject, Ms. Kendall has never taught it before. What steps should she take as she begins to construct her general science curriculum for the year? What will she need to know before she can prepare her lesson plans? What should her daily plans include?

CASE STUDY 5-4

KOUNIN CONCEPTS

As his fourth-period class begins, Mr. Case makes eye contact with two students who are exchanging notes; the students quickly get out their class materials. "Let's begin by working some of the exercises at the end of the chapter; you'll need your notebooks." As students begin to get out their materials, Mr. Case calls out, "Oops, I forgot to tell you to bring money tomorrow for the field trip. How many of you will be going?" After a brief discussion, students finish getting out their materials. Mr. Case says, "We'll go through these exercises orally, but I also want you to write the answers in your notebooks as part of today's classwork. I'll come around and check on your notebook work later in the period. Now, who can answer the first question? Hands please. Tyrone?" Mr. Case conducts the lesson by calling on various students, some with hands up, others seemingly at random from the nonvolunteers. About halfway through the exercises, a student enters the room and says that he is new to the school and has been assigned to the class. Mr. Case goes to his desk, sits down, and says, "Okay, come here. I'll check out a text to you. I wish the school office wouldn't send people in the middle to the period. Where are you from, anyway?" After giving the student a syllabus and a text, Mr. Case leaves his desk and says to the class, "Now where were we? Oh yes, Question 7. Say, where did Kim and Lee go? I didn't give them permission to leave." After several more minutes, Mr. Case calls a halt to the activity and says, "Now I'd like us to discuss the test coming up this Thursday. Let's make sure that you are all clear on what will be on the exam and what you will need to study to get ready for it." After a pause, he adds: "I almost forgot. Get out your questions from before and look at the next to the last one. We need to add an important point that was left out." After finishing the item, Mr. Case turns the topic back to the upcoming test: "Now, where were we. Oh, yes. I need to show you some items that will be similar to those on the test. Here's one." He writes it on the chalkboard, then pauses: "Well, I don't want to give away the test, do I?" Without discussing the test further, he turns to another topic: "Just wait until you hear about the videotape we will be viewing tomorrow. I borrowed it from another teacher, and she said that her students thought it was one of the most thought-provoking, exciting stories they had ever seen!"

 ## CASE STUDY 5-5

A SCIENCE LESSON

After checking roll Ms. Grant tells students that the day's activity will be their first lab assignment and that they will work in groups. "The purpose of the lab work is to get practice with the scientific method," she says, and she lists the stages: observation, formulation of hypothesis, gathering evidence, analysis, and conclusions. Ms. Grant tells students that they must work together in an assigned lab group, and she calls out the group assignments, forming six groups of four or five students each. Students are then told to arrange their desks according to groups. Students are very noisy as they do so, with much playing and talking occurring. Ms. Grant has to speak very loudly in order to regain the students' attention and to give directions for a lab sheet that she distributes to each student. Standing at the front of the room, the teacher reads the directions on the lab sheet while several students continue to converse throughout the instructions. Two groups at the back of the room do not pay attention to the teacher's presentation of directions. Ms. Grant tells students that each group will get a box with something inside and that they should try to determine what it is. They must work together with their partners in the group on the task. having said that, Ms. Grant distributes to each group a small box, wrapped in construction paper. Students immediately treat the boxes as noise makers, causing more commotion. Ms. Grant yells above the din, "Be sure to fill in three guesses at the bottom of the page."

During the ensuing activity only one group discusses what possibilities exist and how they might determine what the box contains. The other groups mainly record the first three guesses that are offered by group members. The teacher observes the groups from a stool at the front of the room. After four minutes she says, "List the tests that you performed. Then put down your three best guesses." After six minutes four of the groups are finished, and students put the boxes back on the teacher's desk. Two groups continue to work on the problem, while the remaining students sit idle or talk. One boy calls out, "When are we going to start?" The teacher responds, "Soon, when everyone is ready." After two more minutes the teacher says, "Listen up, we are ready for the group reports." Some students are still talking while Ms. Grant gives directions for each group's oral report. One student from each group will give the group report, which is to be a statement of each guess and the reasons for it. The teacher also reminds students to follow class rules for listening when other students talk and for not leaving their seats during discussions. "If you can't keep your mouths shut, we won't be able to do activities like this," she notes. While giving reports, students speak softly; it is difficult to hear each report because of talking and fooling around by a number of students. The students' reports are short, and the teacher's comments are limited to brief evaluations and indications of acceptance, such as "Okay," "Good," or "Good observation," Ms. Grant does not record or compare group observations or guesses, but she occasionally asks for clarification, such as, "What makes you guess that?"

After about ten minutes each group report has been given, although many students have not paid attention to any report except the one from their own group. Ms. Grant tells students, "You used a lot of good observations, like the last group that distinguished between round objects and objects with flat sides. Most of the groups were close, and tomorrow I'll tell you what was in each box. Please pass your papers in." After papers have been collected, Ms. Grant asks two students to distribute a classroom set of books. She tells the class to begin reading a chapter on molecules for the next day. After several minutes of commotion, students settle down and read silently for the remaining thirteen minutes of class.

What problems are evident and what changes would be appropriate?

CHECKLIST 5

PLANNING FOR INSTRUCTION

Check When Complete	Before the Lesson, Ask Yourself	Notes
☐	1. What are the most important concepts or skills to be learned?	
☐	2. Are there difficult works or concepts that need extra explanation?	
☐	3. How will you help students make connections to previous learning?	
☐	4. What activities will you plan to create interest in the lesson?	
☐	5. What materials will be needed? Will students need to learn how to use them?	
☐	6. What procedures will students need to follow to complete the activities?	
☐	7. How much time will you allocate for different parts of the lesson?	
☐	8. If activities require students to work together, how will groups be formed? How will you encourage productive work in groups?	
☐	9. What examples and questioning strategies will you use?	
☐	10. How will you tell during and after the lesson what students understand?	
☐	11. What presentation alternatives are there if students have trouble with concepts or skills? Peer explanation, media, textbook, etc.?	
☐	12. Will any students need extra help or more explanation?	
☐	13. How will you make sure that all students participate?	

Check When Complete		Before the Lesson, Ask Yourself	Notes
☐	14.	How will you adjust the lesson if time is too short or long?	
☐	15.	What kind of product, if any, will you expect from students at the end of the lesson?	
☐	16.	What will students do if they finish early?	
☐	17.	How will you evaluate student's performance and give them feedback?	
☐	18.	How will the concepts or skills be used by students in future lessons?	

<table>
<tr><td>

6

</td><td>

Maintaining Appropriate Student Behavior

</td></tr>
</table>

As you have seen in the first five chapters, good classroom management depends on very careful planning of classroom organization, rules, procedures, and instruction. All the preparation will pay large dividends once the students arrive. However, being ready is not sufficient to sustain good behavior throughout the year. You will need to be actively involved in maintaining student cooperation and compliance with necessary classroom rules and procedures. You cannot assume that students will behave appropriately just because you once discussed what was expected of them.

In particular, do not be lulled into complacency by the good behavior of your students during the first few days of school. Most classes are quiet and subdued initially even if the teacher does not pay careful attention to maintaining good behavior, but a class that seems to begin very well may ultimately become disruptive and difficult to control. Behavior problems often have a gradual onset, developing over several weeks or even months. It is usually possible to avoid these problems, but doing so depends on understanding why the problems occur and what to do to prevent them. Because they develop gradually, the causes are not always apparent to the teacher or even to an observer unfamiliar with the history of the classroom.

Teachers who are able to maintain a high level of cooperative, appropriate student behavior often share a number of characteristics and skills. One of these is observant monitoring of students. Such teachers have greater awareness of classroom events and behaviors, which improves their ability to detect and treat problems and help students who are having difficulty. Another characteristic of good managers is consistency in the use of rules and procedures and in their dealings with students who do not follow them. A third attribute is prompt management of inappropriate behavior, before it escalates or spreads. Finally, good behavior is maintained by creating a positive classroom climate, with an emphasis on encouraging appropriate behavior. The remainder of this chapter discusses ways in which these concepts can be implemented.

MONITORING STUDENT BEHAVIOR

To be an effective monitor of classroom behavior, you must know what to look for. Two categories of behavior are especially important:

- Student involvement in learning activities.
- Student compliance with classroom rules and procedures.

Student involvement is indicated by many behaviors, including attention during presentations and discussions and progress in seatwork and other assignments. Students' compliance with classroom rules and procedures will be easy to monitor if you have a clear set of expectations for student behavior and have communicated these to the class.

© Reprinted by permission: Tribune Media Services.

Monitoring student behavior during presentations requires that you stand or sit so that you can see the faces of all the students and that you scan the room frequently. Actively monitoring a class by walking among students tends to increase student attention. Some teachers are not very good monitors of student behavior during whole-class activities because they focus their attention on a limited number of students, especially, those seated in the middle rows and at the front desks. Other teachers "talk to the chalkboard." In either case the teacher does not have a very clear perception of overall student response to the presentation or of what may be occurring at the periphery of the class. During your presentations, therefore, try to move around and develop "active eyes." If you notice commotion involving several students and you have no idea what is going on, this is a sign that you have not been monitoring closely enough.

When students are working on individual assignments, monitoring should be done by circulating around the classroom to check each student's progress periodically and to provide individual feedback. You will, of course, help students who request assistance; however, you should not just "chase hands." If you do, you will not be aware of the progress of all the students. It is very difficult to monitor student progress on assignments from your desk or from any other fixed location, so spend as little time as possible in one location. If you must work at your desk for a time, get up periodically and circulate around the room to check on students' progress and to make sure that directions are being followed correctly. If you must spend a long time (for example, more than a minute or two) helping an individual student, avoid doing it at the student's desk unless you can monitor the rest of the class from that position. For instance, if the student's seat is in the middle of the room, half of the class will be behind you. In such a case call the student to your desk, to the front of the room, or to some other location from which you can easily see all the students. Finally, if for some reason you must work at your desk or at any other location, don't let students congregate around the area. They will obstruct your view of the class, and they may distract students seated nearby. Instead, call students to you one at a time.

A technique for monitoring at the beginning of seatwork that is effective in getting everyone started is to begin the work as a whole-group activity. Have students get out the necessary materials (be sure to look for these on the students' desks), head their papers, and then do the first exercise, or answer the first question or two under your direction. Check and discuss this work with the class. This makes it easy for you to scan the room to be sure that everyone has begun and to determine whether students understand what to do.

A critical monitoring task is checking assignments. Collect them regularly and look them over even when students do the checking in class. Keep your grade book current so that you will be able to detect students who are doing poor work or who skip assignments. If you give a long-term assignment, be sure to check progress regularly. You may even wish to give a grade or assign points toward a grade at these progress checkpoints. You may also have students keep their own checklists of assignments.

CONSISTENCY

The dictum "Be consistent" has been repeated more frequently than the pledge of allegiance. It is still worth some discussion, however, because its meaning is not always clear. In the classroom consistency means retaining the same expectations for behaviors that are appropriate or inappropriate in particular activities; it also means that these expectations apply to every student on all occasions. For example, if students are expected to work silently during seatwork activities on Monday, the same procedure is in effect for all students on Tuesday, Wednesday, and so on. Consistency also applies to the use of penalties. For example, if the penalty for tardy arrival to class is detention, the teacher makes sure that all tardy students receive the penalty and that this procedure is followed even on the days when it is inconvenient to administer it, or in spite of the pleading of individual students that an exception be made. Obvious inconsistency in the use of procedures or in the application of penalties will usually cause students to "test the limits" by not following the procedure or by repeating whatever behavior was to have evoked the penalty. These events can rapidly escalate and force the teacher either to abandon the procedure or to tolerate high levels of inappropriate behavior. Because neither outcome is desirable, it is best to avoid the problem by learning to be consistent in the first place. Of course, it is not possible to be totally consistent, as there will be occasions when the most reasonable course of action will be to make an exception to a rule or procedure. Thus, a deadline for an assignment may be extended when a student has a valid reason, or some procedures might be ignored during an emergency. Note that procedures that are used routinely for some activities but not for others are not inconsistent. For example, you may stipulate that no one leave their seats without permission during discussions or presentations but that during seatwork students are allowed to get materials, sharpen pencils, or turn in papers as needed without permission. As long as you have differentiated between the activities when you explain the procedures to the students, no problems should arise.

Undesirable inconsistency usually arises from three sources. First, the procedures or rules are not reasonable, workable, or appropriate. Second, the teacher fails to monitor students closely and does not detect inappropriate behavior. This gives the appearance of inconsistency when the teacher does detect misbehavior and tries to stop it. Finally, the teacher may not feel strongly enough about the procedure or rule to enforce it or to use the associated penalty. If you find yourself caught in an inconsistency that is becoming a problem, you have the following alternatives:

1. Reteach the procedure. Take a few minutes to discuss the problem with the class and to reiterate your desire that the rule or procedure be followed. Then enforce it.

2. Modify the procedure and then reintroduce it.

3. Abandon the procedure or consequence and possibly substitute another in its place.

The alternative you choose depends on the circumstances and on the importance of the component to your classroom management system.

PROMPT MANAGEMENT OF INAPPROPRIATE BEHAVIOR

Prompt handling of inappropriate behavior is important to avoid its continuation and spread. Behaviors that you should be concerned about include lack of involvement in learning activities, prolonged inattention or work avoidance, and obvious violations of classroom rules and procedures. Effective managers have a high degree of "withitness"; that is, they are so attuned to the class they are able to detect off-task behavior and stop it before it spreads (see Chapter 5 for more discussion of withitness). It is not a good idea to ignore persistent off-task behavior: Prolonged inattention will make it difficult for the students both to learn and to be able to complete assignments; violations of rules and failure to follow procedures create many problems we have already discussed. These behaviors should be dealt with directly, but without overreaction. A calm, reasoned tone or approach will be more productive and less likely to lead to confrontation. The following alternatives are recommended.

Four Ways to Manage Inappropriate Behavior

1. When the student is off-task—that is, not working on an assignment—redirect his or her attention to the task: "Robert, you should be writing now." Or "Becky, the assignment is to complete all the problems on the page." Check the student's progress shortly thereafter to make sure they are continuing to work.

2. Make eye contact with or move closer to the student. Use a signal, such as a finger to the lips or a head shake, to prompt the appropriate behavior. Monitor until the student complies.

3. If the student is not following a procedure correctly, simply reminding the student of the correct procedure may be effective. You can either state the correct procedure or ask the student if he or she remembers it.

4. Ask or tell the student to stop the inappropriate behavior. Then monitor until it stops and the student begins constructive activity.

Sometimes it is inconvenient or would interrupt an activity to use these procedures immediately. In such a case make a mental note of the misbehavior and continue the activity until a more appropriate time occurs. Then tell the student you saw what was occurring, and discuss what the appropriate behavior should have been. Whenever possible, deal with inappropriate behavior privately. Doing so reduces the amount of peer attention the student receives and is less likely to intrude into the ongoing activity.

The four procedures outlined above are easy to use, cause little interruption of class activities, and enable students to correct their behavior. However, if a student persists in the behavior, some other alternatives must be used. If the rest of the class is working and does not need your immediate attention, a brief talk with the student and/or assessing an appropriate penalty may be sufficient. If that doesn't settle the matter or if an immediate conference isn't desirable or feasible, tell the student to wait after class to speak to you. If the student is being disruptive, send him or her to a "time-out" desk in another part of the room, or send the student to the hall. Then talk with the student when you have time. Your goal in discussing the problem behavior with the student is to make clear what the unacceptable behavior is and what the student should be doing, and then to obtain a commitment from the student for acceptable behavior. Some teachers like to have the student put the commitment in writing in a brief "contract" or "plan," specifying what he or she agrees to do, before being allowed to return to class. Additional strategies to deal with problem behaviors are discussed in detail in Chapters 7 and 8, so we will not pursue this topic here.

BUILDING A POSITIVE CLIMATE

This chapter has emphasized maintaining appropriate behavior by applying procedures and rules consistently, handling problems promptly, and using nonintrusive interventions when possible to maintain activity flow and student involvement in lessons. We now want to emphasize the importance of keeping a positive perspective and avoiding overdwelling on student misbehavior or inadequacies. Sometimes teachers get caught in the trap of seeing only faults and problems and overlooking the better features of students' behavior. Instead of rejoicing when twenty-nine students are involved in learning, we complain about the one student who is off-task.

> Mr. Acerbic's ninth-grade physical education class could do no right. Although most of the students initially participated willingly in the class activities, students never seemed to perform quickly or well enough for their teacher. "Come on, you horseflies, quit buzzing and listen up," he would yell when he heard talking. "Laps" around the gym were given for even slight infractions such as inattention; there always seemed to be three or four students making the rounds at any given time. Instead of feedback about good performance, criticism was usually given for inadequacies. Although students took the constant carping in stride, they displayed little zest for the class.

Although poor performance should not be ignored—students need specific, corrective feedback in order to know what they need to improve—it is important that the climate for learning be positive. This means that students should look forward to the class. They should expect to learn and to receive assistance when they encounter difficulty and should feel supported in their efforts. Such a climate can be fostered by communicating positive expectations to students, by praising good performance, and, at times, by using additional rewards.

Teacher expectations can be communicated in a variety of ways, some obvious and others subtle. (For a thorough description of this aspect of teacher behavior, see Good and Brophy, 1987.) Teachers can:

- Identify appropriate instructional goals and discuss them with students so that they are clear about what is expected.

- Insist that students complete work satisfactorily.

- Refuse to accept excuses for poor work.

- Communicate acceptance of imperfect initial performance when students struggle to achieve new learning.

- Convey confidence in the student's ability to do well.

- Display an encouraging, "can do" attitude that generates student excitement and self-confidence.

- Avoid comparative evaluations, especially of lower ability students, that might cause them to conclude that they cannot accomplish the objectives.

By communicating positive expectations, teachers lay the foundation for students to attempt new tasks and reach new goals. When students know that their teacher believes them to be capable, they are more likely to work harder.

A positive climate for learning is also created by appropriate teacher praise. When used well, teacher praise can be uplifting and provide great encouragement to a student. The most powerful type of teacher praise provides the student with information about what aspect of student performance is praiseworthy and also demonstrates that the teacher is impressed with the quality of the student's work. In other words, effective praise provides both informative feedback and genuine teacher approval. It can also accompany suggestions for improvement (constructive criticism), without loss of effect.

Public praise that focuses on student accomplishment works better than praise for student effort. When the teacher praises only for "working hard," students are likely to assume that the teacher thinks they aren't very able. When you know that a student put forth considerable effort and you want to acknowledge it, be sure that the praise also includes an emphasis on the student's achievement. "Gloria, all your hard work paid off, because your project was beautifully done. The organization of ideas and the extra details in the descriptions were outstanding!" Likewise, praise should be deserved and it should not be too easily obtained. Public praise of a student for success on an easy task can suggest to the rest of the class (and the student who was praised) that the teacher believes he or she has little ability.

It is a good idea to look for private ways to provide praise. Written comments on papers, tests, and other assignments offer excellent opportunities for quality praise. Private conversations, conferences with parents, notes home, and informal contacts also offer opportunities for praising students. Private praise avoids some of the complications of public praise, and permits the teacher to include a greater variety of performances and behaviors as the focus of praise. Further discussion of the uses of teacher praise can be found in Emmer (1988) and Brophy (1981).

IMPROVING CLASS CLIMATE THROUGH INCENTIVES OR REWARDS

In some classes extra incentives or rewards can help build a positive climate. The improvement in class climate occurs because the incentives add interest or excitement to the class routine, while also directing attention toward appropriate behavior and away from inappropriate behavior. Moreover, when students are rewarded rather than punished, they are more likely to respond positively to the teacher, contributing to a mutually supportive pattern of interaction.

Before introducing an external incentive, you should consider several factors that might affect its appropriateness and effects. You should check your school or district policies, because sometimes the use of incentives is restricted. You would not want to promise a field trip or party only to find out that it was prohibited by school board policy.

Your rewards should target the behaviors you would like to encourage. Rewards too easily earned or to difficult to achieve lose their motivational effect. Also, you should be concerned about whether the use of a reward takes too much class time for record keeping or other administrative tasks. Avoid using complex systems that distract you and your students from a focus on leaning. Start with simple procedures and add to them if that's reasonable.

Be careful not to set up incentives that only the most able students can achieve. Systems that encourage excessive competition for scarce rewards will discourage those students who don't have much chance. The examples in this section and in the cases at the end of the chapter include a variety of types. Combine these ideas with those of other teachers and your own experience to develop some alternatives for use at various times of the year. Many different types of rewards, including symbols, recognition, activities, and materials, can be used with secondary students. Each of these types is described below with examples.

Grades and Other Symbols

The most prevalent form of this reward is the letter or numerical grade, although other symbols such as checks or stars are sometimes used with students in middle school or junior high school classes. Good grades are a powerful incentive for most students when they are perceived to be a direct reflection of students' achievement, and competence. Therefore, it is important to tie as many facets of student work to grades as possible. In addition, you should make clear to students the basis for determining grades to help them know what they have to do to achieve them. Procedures for student accountability have already been discussed at length in earlier chapters, so we will not dwell upon them here.

One caveat is worth noting. Occasionally teachers react negatively to the grading system because they feel that too much emphasis is placed on grades and not enough on learning. This feeling may cause the teacher to project a casual attitude about grades and to be vague about the grading criteria. This is a mistake; the teacher is still required to assign grades, and the students are left with less control over their fate. A more constructive reaction would be for the teacher to work hard to make the grading criteria reflect the course's learning objectives.

Recognition

These rewards involve some means of giving attention to the student. Examples are the display of student work, awarding a certificate for achievement,

Reprinted by permission: Tribune Media Services.

improvement, or good behavior, and verbally citing student accomplishments. Some adolescents are embarrassed by being singled out for attention, so giving public recognition to several students at the same time is a better strategy. At a school or grade level, recognition awards are often given at the end of the year or semester, with teachers nominating the recipients. If this is the case in your school, be sure to find out what awards are commonly given. Then tell your students what they are (for example, awards for attendance, achievement, improvement, honor students, hard work, conduct, good citizens, and so on) early in the year. Early discussion of these awards may motivate your students to work toward them. A similar procedure is to establish and display an honor roll (for example, an all-star list, honor society, gold record club) to reward students at the end of each grading term. Certificates, stickers with designs appealing to teenagers, or treats can be used in conjunction with the awards, especially for younger secondary students. It is a good idea to spread the honors around to include a good portion of your students. Thus, don't give awards only for outstanding achievement; have awards for improvement, excellent effort, good conduct, and so on.

Activities as Rewards

Permitting or arranging for students to do something special or enjoyable constitutes giving an activity reward. Examples are privileges such as working with a friend, free reading time, visits to the school library, or helping to decorate a bulletin board. A more elaborate activity reward is a field trip or party. Because school policy may affect your use of the latter activities, you should check these out before announcing them to your classes. You should, of course, be certain to describe clearly what students need to do to receive such privileges.

Teachers who use activity rewards as incentives for the whole class can permit students to participate in their identification and selection. Thus, a list of possibly desirable (and acceptable) activities can be presented to a class or solicited from students during a discussion; either way, the class can vote on whichever one it wishes to seek. Some whole-class activities that might be used include watching a videotape, fifteen minutes of free time, playing games, listening to music, having a popcorn party, or no homework. A group activity reward should be made contingent on specific desirable behaviors; if the group cooperates, then they receive the incentive. If not, then they lose some or all of the time in the activity. Because the purpose of using an activity reward is, at least in part, to promote positive climate building, it is important not to let one or two students spoil the fun for the rest of the class. A chronically uncooperative student or two can be invited to participate in the system, but if they persist in noncompliance the teacher may exclude them from the system. Of course, they should be encouraged to participate and given the opportunity to make that choice.

Finding a supervised place for the excluded student during the activity is a limitation of using this incentive. Sometimes teachers solve the problem by arranging ahead of time for the student to go to another teacher's classroom. The student then works on assigned seatwork during the time. It is best if the receiving class is not at the same grade level as the excluded student, in order to reduce the potential for interaction or undue attention from peers.

Material Incentives

These rewards include awarding objects of value to students. Examples include food, money, discarded classroom materials, games, toys, or books. In addition to ascertaining school policy, you will have to consider your own financial circumstances before deciding to use such rewards. Because you will have a large number of students and limited resources, your use of material rewards will be restricted at best.

When you consider what types of rewards to use in your classes, several factors should be kept in mind. Your rewards should be related to the student behaviors that are most important to you. Obviously, one such set of student behaviors is satisfactory completion of assignments, participation in academic activities, and attainment of learning objectives. For these student behaviors grades are effective and relevant rewards. Another set of important student behaviors are those related to following rules and major procedures. For these behaviors recognition and activity rewards can be used effectively. Some teachers hold competitions among their different class sections, rewarding the class that has the best behavior record, attendance record, or homework completion rate for a grading period. With the cooperation of other teachers and administrators, good student behavior can be rewarded by a party or dance at the end of the semester for all students who have stayed off the detention list and maintained good attendance records. An incentive on such a grand scale requires much planning and effort as well as the cooperation of large numbers of people.

Caution in the Use of Rewards

Some researchers (e.g., Deci and Ryan, 1985; Lepper and Greene, 1978) have urged caution in the use of extrinsic rewards, pointing out that under some circumstances their use may reduce students' intrinsic motivation to engage in the rewarded activity. In studies conducted by motivational researchers, subjects are given a reward for engaging in an activity or for reaching some predetermined level of performance. Later the reward is withdrawn and the subjects are observed when they are free to choose the activity and how long to engage in it. Compared to subjects who do not receive an external incentive, the previously rewarded subjects tend to choose other activities more or to engage in the rewarded activity for a shorter time. From such results it is inferred that receiving a reward reduces motivation for an activity if subsequently the extrinsic reward is no longer available.

Explanations of this dampening effect on motivation usually focus on the thinking processes that occur when individuals are given rewards. "This is an unpleasant or boring task, so a reward is needed to maintain engagement," is the implicit message communicated by the use of external rewards. Consequently, the recipient tends to devalue the rewarded activity.

Before concluding that teachers should never use incentives, however, it should be noted that research in this area has a number of limitations with respect to its generalization to classroom practice. For one thing, much of the research has been conducted in laboratory settings in which the activity or task and its accompanying reward occur on only one occasion; in addition, the rewarded activity or task has usually been a highly interesting one, such as a game or puzzle. Thus, the research setting and the tasks are often not very representative of the nature

Calvin and Hobbes   by Bill Watterson

of classroom work for which rewards might usually be used. Furthermore, some research has found that incentives can enhance interest, rather than reduce it. Bandura (1986) argues that the conflicting findings mean that the effect of extrinsic rewards on intrinsic motivation is weak and that many other factors operate to mediate the effects of the use of incentives.

We believe that the most reasonable application of the research results for classroom use of rewards is to be thoughtful about their use. No purpose will be served by adding a reward to an activity that is already highly interesting to students, and the evidence strongly suggests that to do so will often cause reduced motivation. However, many classroom tasks are not highly interesting, especially during the extensive repetition that is needed to produce skilled performance and learning. When student motivation flags, external incentives will be necessary to maintain engagement. In fact, the use of incentives is much more desirable than lowering expectations and accepting poor performance, or using punishment and threats to attempt to keep students working. Finally, when rewards are used, the teacher can counteract the potential for negative effects on intrinsic motivation by pointing out the usefulness of the skill, by choosing materials and activities that have more potential for sustaining student interest, by pointing out to students that the reward is not the only thing "fun" about the activity and that it will lead to long-term outcomes of value to the students, and by demonstrating personal interest and enthusiasm in the task.

SUGGESTED ACTIVITIES

1. Read the descriptions of incentives in Case Study 6-1 and consider whether and how you might adapt the ideas to your classes.

2. Find out about school policies that affect your use of rewards and penalties. Also, note any schoolwide system that you will need to incorporate into your own classroom's procedures.

CASE STUDY 6-1

EXAMPLES OF INCENTIVES AND REWARDS

Some additional examples of incentives and rewards that we have observed in secondary school classrooms are described in the following pages. These examples are grouped according to type, although it should be noted that some incentives combine features of several types.

Awards and Other Recognition. An attractive award certificate was designed by a teacher and used for individual students at different times during the year. The certificates were especially impressive because each was signed by the principal as well as the teacher. Students were recognized for outstanding effort, improvement, or accomplishment. To save time the teacher made many copies of the blank certificates before school began and asked the principal to sign them all at once. She filled them in as needed with students' names and accomplishments. The certificates were awarded both publicly and privately, according to the student and the accomplishment. (Note: Blank achievement/appreciation certificates can also be purchased from school supply stores.)

Honor roll systems are commonly used at the secondary level. Generally, these school-wide systems have incentive value for better students and don't provide much motivation for the less academically successful. One teacher who taught several classes of low achievers in a school that used ability grouping developed an in-class honor roll that was more accessible to his students. At the end of each grading period, students who had improved their performance or who had participated well in class activities were named to a "Best in the West" honor roll. Their names were placed on a bulletin board honor roll, and they received attractive stickers to display on their notebooks or textbook covers.

Competitions. For some subjects long-range incentives are available in the form of city, regional, or statewide competitions (for example, spelling or composition contests, science and math fairs). Other competitions can be conducted within a school, with classes competing against each other, or they may even be limited to the classes taught by one teacher. The teacher can establish a reward for the first class completing a project or for the class in which all students complete the project first. Within-class rewards can also be offered. One teacher posted spelling grades by class on a bulletin board display. The class with the highest overall score at the end of each month received a special prize or treat.

Encouraging Improvement. Some teachers allow students to redo incorrectly done assignments to improve their grade. Students might be allowed to earn enough points to bring their grade up to a B level, for example. One teacher kept a chart on which stars were placed representing students' grades on assignments. For example, a gold star stood for an A, a silver star for a B, and so on. No star meant that the assignment had not been turned in. If a student redid an assignment and brought up its grade, the teacher placed a different color star on top of the previous star. Displaying the chart on a bulletin board also encouraged students to do their best and to avoid missing assignments.

Extra-Credit Assignments. Extra-credit activities are frequently popular with students, and the extra credit earned toward improving a grade is an important incentive for most students. One teacher kept an extra-credit logic problem on the side board, changing it every week or two depending on its difficulty. She also had extra-credit puzzles and worksheets on a front table. These puzzles covered material currently being studied by the class, and students were encouraged to work on these after they had finished their required work. They could also copy them and work on them at home. This teacher had students keep their completed extra-credit problems in a special section of their notebooks, where they were checked when the teacher graded the notebooks. Each correct problem was worth one point and was added to the notebook grade at the end of the grading period.

A science teacher kept a list of extra-credit projects for students to work on individually or in groups. Along with the list of projects was a description of the requirements for each project, its complexity, a deadline for completion, and the number of points earned toward a report card grade. English and social studies teachers frequently have book lists from which students may choose extra-credit reading. A form for students to use when reporting on the book should also be available.

Sometimes bulletin boards are used to display extra-credit work. One math teacher had a picture of a mountain, with math problems relevant to current lessons at each of several elevations. Beneath the mountain were lines for ten student names. The first ten students (from all classes) correctly completing the problems had their names posted under the mountain. When the tenth name was posted, the teacher taped a piece of gum or candy beside each name for the student to remove.

Special Activities and Privileges. Allowing students special privileges or permitting them to participate in desired activities is a commonly used reward, and it is often combined with another kind of reward such as recognition. For example, one teacher chose outstanding students each week, based on their attitude, grades, and attendance. The teacher would put students' names on a bulletin board display, and students would receive a special treat on Friday. The teacher also included in the special activity or treat all students who had not received demerits for misbehavior during that week. Another teacher recognized consistent performance by naming all students who had turned in all their work during the previous week as a "Student of the Week" and by placing their names on a special bulletin board display. After being named "Student of the Week" five times during a six-week grading period, the student was entitled to claim an A for one of the four major components of the report card grade. One teacher allowed fifteen or twenty minutes of free reading or game time on Friday when a class had been well behaved throughout the week. Another teacher made an "activity chain" from construction paper, adding a link when class behavior was good each day. When the chain reached a certain length, the class was permitted to have part of a period for a special activity such as free reading or a class competition.

Weekly Point System.   Point systems are useful because in addition to giving students clearly specified incentives, they encourage students to take responsibility for keeping track of their own work. One teacher gave a handout to students at the beginning of each week, with the week's assignments on it. The students recorded points they earned for each assignment, with up to 100 points awarded weekly. Some bonus points were also available for extra-credit assignments, and the teacher could add extra points for good behavior and class participation. These weekly records of points were then used along with test scores to determine report card grades.

<table>
<tr><td>

7

</td><td>

Communication Skills for Teaching

</td></tr>
</table>

Throughout this book we have emphasized classroom management's preventive and instructional aspects. Not all problems can be prevented, however, and sometimes unobtrusive handling of inappropriate behavior during instruction is not sufficient. The approaches described in this chapter provide some additional means for dealing with problems that persist. The example below illustrates such a situation.

> During the past several days Debra and Diane have been increasingly inattentive in Ms. Harris' fifth-period class. Their off-task behavior has included whispering with other students and each other, teasing boys seated nearby, and displaying exaggerated boredom with class discussions. Ms. Harris first asked the girls to stop bothering the class, and when that had no effect, she moved the girls to different seats. However, Debra and Diane continued to disrupt by passing notes and calling out loudly to one another.

We will not second-guess Ms. Harris by wondering whether she had communicated expectations clearly or had taken action promptly enough; let us suppose that she had, in fact, practiced good preventive management skills but that the students misbehaved anyway. No strategy works all the time. What options are now available to Ms. Harris to deal with the situation? Some possible approaches include the following:

- Ignore the problem and hope it goes away.
- Refer the students to an assistant principal.
- Call the students' parents and ask for their help.
- Apply a consequence, such as detention or some other punishment.

Each of the above approaches has advantages and limitations. For example, ignoring the problem requires little effort and might work if the students are mainly seeking teacher attention. The description does not, however, suggest that this is a likely reason for the behavior, and ignoring may only allow it to intensify and spread to other students. Referral has the advantage of demanding little of the teacher's time, at least in the short run; it also temporarily removes the disruptive students, and it can have deterrent value. However, it may do nothing in the long run to deal with the problem the students are causing in the class, and although referral may sometimes be a reasonable approach to serious misbehavior, it can easily be overused.

A telephone call to parents sometimes works wonders and is usually worth a try. However, parents cannot always stop misbehavior. They do not, after all, accompany their child to your class, nor do they control the cues that are eliciting the misbehavior. Punishing the students by assigning detention or withholding some desirable activity or privilege is another possible reaction. Punishment, can stop misbehavior, at least temporarily, and it can deter other students. But punishment can have the disadvantages of creating hostility or resentment and of trapping the teacher and students in a cycle of misbehavior-reaction that leads to power struggles. By itself, punishment does little to teach the student self-control and responsibility.

Because each of these approaches has limitations, you need additional means of coping with problems. This does not mean that other approaches such as ignoring, referral, applying consequences, or involving parents will be supplanted. It does mean that communication strategies should be added to your repertoire to deal with problems that cannot be corrected with minor inventions and to help students learn to take responsibility for their own behavior.

In addition to being helpful when dealing with students whose behavior is creating a problem for the teacher or for other students, communication skills can be used to assist students who are themselves experiencing problems. Teachers frequently become aware of students' problems caused by factors both inside and outside the classroom. Teachers can help these students by being good listeners and by encouraging them to consider alternate ways to solve problems or to adapt to difficult situations.

We use the label *communication skills* for the set of strategies described in this chapter to emphasize that the approach focuses on communicating clearly and effectively with students to help bring about a change in their behavior, in their thinking, or in the situation that has caused the problem. In addition, communication also means being open to information, so teachers also need to be good listeners and to try to understand the student's (or parent's) concerns and feelings. In order to become an effective communicator, three related skills are needed:

1. **Constructive assertiveness.** This includes describing your concerns clearly, insisting that misbehavior be corrected, and resisting being coerced or manipulated.

2. **Empathic responding.** This refers to listening to the student's perspective and reacting in ways that maintain a positive relationship and encourage further discussion.

3. **Problem solving.** This component includes several steps for reaching mutually satisfactory resolutions to problems; it requires working with the student to develop a plan for change.

The three elements are derived from a variety of sources, including Gordon's *Teacher Effectiveness Training*, Gazda's *Human Relations Development: A Manual for Educators*, Glasser's *Reality Therapy*, Alberti's *Assertiveness*, Zuker's *Mastering Assertiveness Skills*, and other standard references. These books are listed in the bibliography. The treatment of communication skills in this chapter is intended to be an introduction; if you are interested in further reading, we suggest that you refer to one or more of the cited books.

Although this chapter's treatment of assertiveness, empathic responding, and problem solving focuses on their use with students, the skills are very helpful when dealing with parents—especially during parent conferences—and other adults. Thus, the skills described in this chapter have a variety of applications and will improve your effectiveness in handling many classroom and school-related situations.

CONSTRUCTIVE ASSERTIVENESS

Assertiveness is the ability to stand up for one's legitimate rights in ways that make it less likely that others will ignore or circumvent them. The adjective *constructive* implies that the assertive teacher does not tear down or attack the student. It can be thought of as a general characteristic or attribute that is used in a wide variety of settings or as a set of skills that are more situation specific. Some individuals are assertive in an array of situations (e.g., interacting with strangers, on the job, at parties, in school, etc.), while others lack assertiveness in many of these settings.

However, even if you are not generally assertive, you can learn to use assertive behaviors while you are teaching. In fact, doing so may help generalize the behaviors to other situations as you become more confident of your skills. People who are very unassertive (e.g., they feel very nervous whenever they are expected to lead a group; they are unable to begin conversations or to make eye contact with others; they accede to inappropriate demands readily; they are unable to ask others to respect their rights) will find teaching uncomfortable and will have particular difficulty with discipline. Such persons can help themselves in several ways, especially by reading about assertiveness and practicing some of the skills, preferably in situations that are not too uncomfortable, until they begin to develop confidence. It is also possible to obtain professional help, such as from a counseling center, or to enroll in a course or workshop on assertiveness training. A good assertiveness training program will usually include anxiety-reduction exercises, skills training and practice in developing more effective behaviors, and cognitive restructuring to reshape negative thought patterns that interfere with appropriate social interaction.

The elements of constructive assertiveness include:

- A clear statement of the problem or issue
- Unambiguous body language
- Insistence on appropriate behavior and resolution of the problem

Assertiveness is not:

- Hostile or aggressive
- Argumentative
- Inflexible
- Wimpy, wishy-washy, doormat behavior

Assertiveness lies on a continuum between aggressive, overbearing pushiness and timid, submissive, or weak responses that allow students to trample on the teacher's and other students' rights. By using assertiveness skills you communicate to students that you are serious about teaching and about maintaining a classroom in which everyone's rights are respected.

Assertiveness has three basic elements:

- *A clear statement of the problem or concern.* Student misbehavior usually causes problems for teachers by making it difficult to conduct lessons, by slowing down activities, and by subverting routines that help a class run smoothly. When misbehavior persists, it is time for the teacher to let the student know what the problem is, from the teacher's point of view. Sometimes just a simple description of the problem is enough to produce behavior change, because the student becomes more aware of the behavior and begins to monitor it better. Stating the problem has two parts: (1) identifying the student behavior and (2) describing its effects, if they are not obvious:

"Talking and passing notes during discussion distracts other students from the lesson."

"Calling out answers without raising your hand prevents others from participating."

"Wandering around the room disturbs the class."

"Calling other students names causes hard feelings."

By focusing on the behavior and its effects you can reduce the potential for student defensiveness and keep open the opportunity for achieving a satisfactory resolution.

Notice that the problem descriptions above avoid labeling either students or their behavior; i.e., accusing them of being bad, rude, and annoying or behaving in an inconsiderate or infantile manner. Labeling should be avoided because it interferes with behavior change by communicating a negative expectation that the student might accept as valid. Notice also that statements rather than questions are used. Quizzing students (e.g., "Why are you talking?" "Do you think that you should be calling someone that name?") invites defensive, sarcastic, or oppositional responses and can result in arguments.

- *Body language.* Constructive assertiveness with students needs to be reinforced by appropriate body language in three areas. The first is making eye contact when addressing the student, especially when describing the problem and when calling for behavior change. Note that there is a difference between eye contact that communicates seriousness and resolve versus an angry glare that emits hostility. In the former case, breaking eye contact from time to time relieves tension. A second area of assertive body language is maintaining an erect posture facing the student (but not so close as to appear to threaten), to communicate your attention and involvement in the conversation. A third area is matching your facial expressions with the content and tone of your statements (e.g., not smiling when making serious statements).
- *Obtaining appropriate behavior.* Assertiveness requires that the teacher not be diverted from insisting on appropriate behavior. Students may deny involvement, argue, or blame others (including the teacher). When dealing with such diversionary tactics remember, "There are many reasons for misbehavior, but

no excuses." While it is possible that others contributed to the problem, the student needs to accept responsibility for his or her behavior. It is important to listen carefully to and understand the student's situation, but in the end, if the student's behavior is interfering with your ability to teach, the behavior must change. Thus, if a student begins to argue or to deny responsibility for the behavior, you should avoid being sidetracked.

When working with students who are evasive or who are not taking matters very seriously, a little dramatic emphasis may help move them to reconsider the situation. Consider Ms. Harris during a conference with Debra and Diane:

> "I've asked you to stay after class because I'm very concerned with the behavior in the fifth period. Please sit down." (Pauses, looks at the girls.) "I had to stop class three times today because of your loud talking." (Rises from behind desk, voice slightly louder.) "I cannot teach when noise interferes with our discussions." (Sits down, looks at the girls.) "This cannot go on any more." (Calmer) "I would like us to work out a solution to this problem. Do you think we can?"

Being an assertive teacher means that you let students know your concerns and needs in a manner that gets their attention and communicates your intent to carry through with consequences and to deal with the situation until it is resolved. It is not necessary that you lose your sense of humor or treat students impolitely. A little humor can reduce tension, and treating students with courtesy models the kind of behavior that you expect of them. Developing a level of assertiveness that is comfortable for you and understanding how your behavior is perceived by others are important. Working through activities presented at the end of the chapter will help develop your skills and self-awareness.

EMPATHIC RESPONDING

Another important communication skill is the ability to respond with empathy to students. This skill allows you to show you are aware and accepting of the student's perspective as well as to seek clarification of it when necessary. Empathic responding helps keep the lines of communication open between you and students, so that problems can be understood and resolved in mutually acceptable ways. Such skills are especially appropriate when students express their concerns, show stress, or display other strong emotions. As a teacher you should respond in a manner that helps the student deal constructively with those feelings, or at least avoids adding to the student's discomfort or distress. Empathic responding can also be used as a part of the problem-solving process when dealing with students who must change their behavior. In such situations, students can be resistant and express negative feelings; the teacher's empathic responses can help defuse these reactions and increase acceptance of a plan for change.

Empathic responding complements constructive assertiveness. Whereas assertiveness allows teachers to express their concerns, empathic responding solicits and affirms the student's viewpoint. The use of empathic responding skills does not imply that misbehaving students are entitled to "do their thing" without regard for others; rather, the implication is that the student's views should be taken into account in order to reach a satisfactory solution. If the teacher shows some openness to the student's perspective, there is a better chance that the student will make a commitment to change. Conversely, a teacher who shows no interest in the student's feelings is more likely to encounter defiant behavior and an unwillingness to cooperate or to accept responsibility.

Compare the following two episodes.

Episode A

Student: I'm not staying. You can't make me.
Teacher: You'll have to stay after school. You've been tardy three times.
Student: Oh man, I can't stay.
Teacher: That's life. If you don't serve your time now, it's doubled. That's the rule.
Student: (*Angry*) I'm leaving.
Teacher: You'd better not.
Student: Buzz off! (*Student leaves.*)

In the above episode, the teacher's response does nothing to resolve the situation. It's likely that the student is aware of the consequences of skipping detention, so the argument only provokes a confrontation which the student wins, at least temporarily, by leaving.

Another way to handle the situation is illustrated below.

Episode B

Student: I'm not staying. You can't make me.
Teacher: I agree. It's up to you.
Student: I can't stay.
Teacher: Staying after school is a problem for you?
Student: I can't be late to practice.
Teacher: Oh, I see. The detention would make you late for practice.

> *Student:* Right, and if I'm late one more time, I'll have to sit out the next game.
>
> *Teacher:* That's a difficult situation. What are your options?

In Episode B, the teacher avoids arguing with the student and instead acknowledges the student's concern and invites further discussion. The student responds to the teacher's approach by stating his or her concern more explicitly. Notice that the teacher's role in this conference is that of listener or helper, rather than opponent. Notice, too, that the teacher does not offer to solve the student's problem by dropping the detention penalty. Instead, the student is led to consider what options are available. Of course, there is no guarantee that the situation will be resolved to everyone's satisfaction. Yet, the approach at least offers the possibility of resolution, and it avoids the confrontation that occurred in Episode A. Further, it maintains the student's responsibility for dealing with the situation rather than giving the student yet another excuse for avoiding responsibility.

Empathic responding has several advantages. It provides the teacher a means of dealing with strong emotions, without taking over responsibility for solving the student's problems. At the same time, the strategy helps defuse emotionally charged situations: Often, intense feelings are transient and will persist only when fed by an intense response. By not responding with similar emotional intensity, the teacher avoids fueling the fire. Also, the calm, empathic teacher will serve as a good model for constructive problem solving.

Empathic responding has two components: listening skills and processing skills.

Listening skills acknowledge or accept the student's expression of feeling or ideas and are intended to encourage students to continue discussing the situation. At a minimal level, the listener merely indicates attention. Sometimes, just an interested look and a nod will encourage the student to continue speaking. Other examples of nonverbal listening behaviors are nodding, making eye contact with the speaker, and other body language that communicates openness to discussion. Verbal encouragement is indicated by utterances such as "Um-hm," "I see," "Go on," "That's interesting," and the like. At other times a little more encouragement may be needed. In such a case the teacher can invite more discussion with phrases such as, "Tell me more," "I'm interested in hearing your ideas about this," "Would you care to comment?" "What do you think?" and "You've listened to my opinion. I'd like to listen to yours."

Processing skills allow you to confirm or clarify your perception of the student's message. At the simplest level you can just repeat back or summarize what the student says. When the student has provided multiple messages or a confusing array of statements, you can select what seems to be most important and paraphrase it. You can then "reflect" or "bounce back" this paraphrase as a question. Often, the student will acknowledge the correctness of your perception or offer clarification. For example, consider this interchange from a short after-school conference:

Student: I hate this place. School is stupid!

Teacher: Would you like to talk about it?

Student: I just don't like it here.

Teacher: School really turns you off.

Student: No. Not school, I mean here, this place.

Teacher: You like some schools, but not this high school?

Student: Right, there's too many rules, no one listens to you, you can't talk to your friends. You know, it's just do this, do that, shut up.

Teacher: You feel too restricted here, like you can't do what you want and no one cares?

Student: It's always teachers telling you to be quiet, do your work. There's never time to be with friends and to have fun.

Teacher: It sounds like you'd like more opportunities to socialize and hang out.

Student: Right. If I could only have some things to look forward to, that I'd feel like coming here for, it'd be more bearable.

Teacher: I wonder if you're aware of the activities we have after school . . .

In the example, the teacher uses a variety of responses with a turned-off student and progresses to a point where the student can express, at least partially, some of the basis for the feelings. Note that as the discussion unfolds the student becomes more communicative and reasonable. Although one cannot expect that major problems will usually be resolved via a single empathic interchange, it is not unusual for the sharp edge of negative emotions to be blunted and for the conversation to end on a positive note. At the least, the student will know that an adult cares enough to listen and the teacher will be in a better position to guide the student in the future.

The skills of empathic responding—both listening and processing—have been presented in the context of interactions with individual students, but they are also helpful when problems arise in group settings. In particular, using these tactics helps prevent teachers from responding defensively when students react emotionally or express a problem during class. They also "buy time" for the teacher to consider alternatives for dealing with a problem. In addition, listening and processing skills are useful for leading group discussions.

Although empathic responding skills are very helpful in some situations, they are not intended as the primary means of dealing with students who are acting out, breaking class rules, or interfering with other students. Such misbehavior needs to be dealt with using approaches discussed in Chapters 6 and 8 and in the other sections of this chapter. However, listening and processing can be used to support these other measures.

Another limitation in the use of these skills is that of finding the right time and place to use them. It would be awkward, to say the least, to respond empathically to every expression of emotion or opinion during class activities. Such reactivity would cause slowdowns and might undermine your students' attention to lessons. How frequently and in which circumstances you choose to use these skills will depend on a variety of factors, including opportunities, your goals and values, and how competent you feel.

PROBLEM SOLVING

Problem solving is a process that is used to deal with and to resolve conflicts. Conflicts arise between teachers and students because different roles give rise to different needs, and because individuals have different goals and interests. If conflict arises, teachers need a way to manage it constructively so that teaching and learning can continue in a supportive classroom climate. An effective means of accomplishing this is the problem-solving process, in which the teacher works with the student to develop a plan to reduce or eliminate the problem. Steps in the process include (1) identification of the problem, (2) discussion of alternative solutions, and (3) obtaining a commitment to try one of them. Depending on circumstances, a problem-solving session may also include attempts to identify the basis for the problem and may specify the consequences of following or not following the plan. Because it generally requires more than a brief intervention, a problem-solving session is usually conducted during a conference with the student. Often, the skills of constructive assertiveness and empathic responding are helpful in reaching a workable agreement.

Problem-solving conferences are usually reserved for chronic situations that have not yielded to simpler remedies. Some action needs to be taken to stop the behavior, because allowing it to continue would interfere with your ability to teach, with other students' opportunities to learn, or with the student's long-term functioning in your class or school.

Consider the following examples.

1. Brad likes to be the center of attention. Whenever you ask a question he calls out the answer without raising his hand and with no regard for the fact that you have already called on another student. Although you have reminded him of correct behavior and have tried to ignore his call-outs, the behavior continues to interfere with your class discussions.

2. Alice and Alicia always seem to be in a hurry to leave your room at the end of the fourth period. Unfortunately, they do not clean up their art

supplies and they fuss and argue when you have them return to finish their jobs. Then they complain they will be late to their next class. Their foot dragging seemed trivial at first, but it has become a daily source of irritation that disrupts the last several minutes of the class each day.

3. Terrence has not turned in his last three assignments, even though you allowed ample time in class to work on them. He seems to have a lackadaisical attitude about academic work, and he uses his time in class for goofing off whenever he can get away with it. During the previous grading period he was within one point of failing your course, and not turning in his work is sure to drop him below the failing point.

Each of the above examples illustrates a situation that has reached a stage at which a problem-solving conference might be useful. In each case, routine intervention has not affected the student's behavior; in each case, more of the same teacher response will only result in a continuing power struggle or in a deterioration in the student's ability to behave constructively.

What is evident in each example is that the students are not accepting responsibility for their behavior. Perhaps what is needed is a stronger consequence (e.g., a penalty) that is clearly contingent on a repetition of the misbehavior. In fact, this strategy can be an alternative discussed with students during a problem-solving conference. But until the students make a commitment to change the offending behavior, the use of punishment may be perceived as coercive and controlling, rather than as a logical consequence of their behavior, and thus may do little or no good. It also appears that the basis of the problems in each of the three examples is not clear. Why won't Brad wait his turn? Why can't Alicia and Alice follow the simple clean-up procedure? Doesn't Terrence understand or care about what will happen to his grade? Giving the students a chance to discuss their situations might produce insights that would lead to better solutions. It would also permit the teacher and students to become more aware of each other's perceptions and possibly prevent the development of additional problems.

Steps in a problem-solving conference are described below.

Step 1: *Problem identification.* You can begin the discussion by stating the purpose of the meeting and asking the student to express his or her viewpoint. Obtaining the student's view provides useful information for later steps and it also enables you to gauge the student's understanding of the situation and willingness to cooperate. An alternative opening is to describe the problem yourself and ask the student for a reaction; this alternative will be especially needed when dealing with young children, with students having limited verbal skills, and with evasive and dissembling students. Unless the student's attitude is very cooperative you need to be assertive about expressing your concerns, As explained earlier this can be done by describing, without labeling, the behavior of concern and the problem it is causing. You may also need to stress that the problem will not be allowed to continue, and that something must be done to solve it.

Glasser (as cited in Basser, Bratter, and Rachin, 1976) recommends asking students to evaluate whether the behavior is helping or hurting them, or has good or bad effects. The logic is that a student who understands and admits that a behavior has negative consequences will be more likely to participate in the search for and commitment to a solution. A student who denies responsibility or who sees no harmful effects seldom makes a meaningful commitment to change. It may be helpful to ask such a student what the consequences might be if the behavior continues.

During this initial phase of the conference, a student may react defensively or emotionally and may try to avoid responsibility by blaming others, arguing, citing extenuating circumstances, and so forth. When such behaviors occur, you must decide whether the student's reaction is primarily for the purpose of evading responsibility or if it has some validity. If the latter is the case, then you can use listening and processing skills to respond; this communicates a willingness to hear the student's point of view and may increase subsequent cooperation. Again, there is considerable reciprocity in interaction, and if you model desirable behavior, you encourage its use by the student. A disadvantage of using empathic responding during this phase of problem solving is that the student's excuses, arguments, and extenuating circumstances may simply be a means of avoiding responsibility. Because you do not want to get sidetracked from the issue that brought the student to the conference in the first place, be sure to return the focus to the main problem once student concerns have been expressed. When the problem has been identified and agreed upon, the conference can move to the next step.

Step 2: *Identifying and selecting a solution.* One way to begin this phase is to invite the student to suggest a solution to the problem. If the student is unable to do so, then you can offer one. Whenever possible, it is best to have two or more alternatives, so that options can be compared and the most desirable one chosen. Frequently, the student's solution will be stated negatively, focusing on simply ending an undesirable behavior. While this is a step in the right direction, it is best to include a positive focus as well, by including a plan for increasing desirable behavior. Thus, you should be ready to work with the student's idea and also to suggest modifications.

If you are the one who suggests a solution, seek the student's reaction in order to check whether the plan is understood and accepted. Also, evaluate the plan's appropriateness: Is it realistic? Will it significantly reduce the problem?

Does it call for changes in other students or in the classroom environment and are such changes feasible? Can it be evaluated readily? Occasionally a student may try to avoid responsibility by proposing a solution that places the burden for change upon the teacher or other students, e.g., to design more interesting lessons or to get other students to "leave me alone." Consider such changes to the extent they are appropriate and reasonable, but don't allow a student to shift responsibility to others unless that is where the responsibility for the problem lies. A reasonable response is, "Yes, such changes might help, but what will you contribute?" Once a mutually agreeable solution is reached, you are ready for the third stage.

> Step 3: *Obtaining a commitment.* In this step the teacher asks the student to accept the solution and to try it for a specified period of time, usually with the understanding that it will be evaluated afterward. The student's commitment can be given verbally or in written form, as in a "contract." Sometimes such contracts are printed with an official-looking border, seal, and script, with space for student and teacher signatures and for listing contract terms and consequences if the plan is or is not followed.

Whether or not consequences are specified will depend on the severity of the problem and whether it is a first conference or a follow-up for a broken contract. Some teachers like to give students a chance to correct their behavior without resorting to penalties; the rationale is that long-range cooperation is better when the teacher uses the least controlling or coercive approach. However, if the student is not making a reasonable effort to comply with the plan, or if the misbehavior is dangerous or too disruptive to be allowed to continue, then spelling out the consequences may well be needed to get the student's attention and to communicate the seriousness of the situation: "You will need to choose between following our agreement or discussing your behavior with the assistant principal—Mr. Dreadnaught—and your parents."

If the plan fails to solve the problem, then you'll either need to follow through with whatever consequence was stipulated, or else you'll need to work with the student to alter the plan to produce a more workable solution. A major consideration is how much time and energy you can or should devote to pursuing the plan, versus using a referral, detention, or some other consequence available in your school. You might also consult with a counselor, assistant principal, or another teacher before taking further action in order to get another perspective on the problem.

When problem-solving conferences fail to make progress (e.g., the student does not make a sincere commitment to a plan or simply does not cooperate), the teacher should evaluate his or her assertiveness and empathic responding skills before concluding that a problem-solving approach does not work with that student. Poor assertiveness skills—hostile, critical, or attacking behaviors—and their opposite—timid, tentative responding—will interfere with the problem-solving process. An overly assertive, hostile style reflects a reliance on the teacher's power and cuts off communication. An unassertive style is easily ignored; the teacher is not seen as credible, and students simply won't believe that the teacher will insist on correct behavior or will follow through with consequences if they push past the limits. A constructively assertive teacher, however, captures the students' attention and communicates serious intent to change the situation. Empathic responding communicates a willingness to listen to the student's point of view and permits the teacher to clarify and react to a student's statements without closing off further discussion. Such skills are especially needed during problem-solving discussions because they allow the teacher to deal constructively with defensive student behavior. They also help to clarify solutions as they are discussed and to improve the chances of obtaining a sincere commitment to change.

When you use these skills, be patient and give them a chance to work. Often teachers use a problem-solving approach after a situation has reached a flashpoint or for behavior that has been established over a long period of time. In such cases, you cannot expect miracles; change may occur gradually and imperfectly. However, problem-solving conferences can be helpful in many cases and should be a component of your set of management and discipline skills.

Examples of problem-solving conferences are presented in Case Studies 7-1 and 7-2. In addition, exercises on problem solving are presented in the activities.

SUGGESTED ACTIVITIES

Activity 7-1: Developing Assertiveness Skills.   The purpose of this activity is to provide some situations for practicing assertiveness skills. For each situation described below, prepare an assertive response. Use the following sequence of steps with each situation until you are comfortable with the approach. Then combine the steps so that you have the experience of responding to situations "on your feet."

Step 1: Write out a statement that describes the problem clearly or that insists that your rights be respected. Compare and discuss your statements with other participants. Revise your statement if you wish.

Step 2: Use role playing to portray the situation, with you as teacher and someone else as the student. During the role play, try to use appropriate body language (eye contact, facial expression) to support your intervention.

Step 3: Get feedback from observers regarding your use of assertiveness skills. Use the Assertiveness Scales to assess your own behavior, and check out your perceptions by comparing your self ratings to those of observers. Be sure to discuss any discrepancies and any problems you experienced enacting an assertive role. Repeat Step 2 until you feel comfortable with your handling of the situation.

It is not necessary to continue the role play to a complete resolution of the situation. The purpose is only to provide experience in enacting assertive behaviors. The person playing the student role should respond as naturally as possible.

- *Situation A.* Bubba has been sliding by lately, doing the minimum and barely passing. At the end of class today he asks you if it would be all right to turn in his project a few days late. He knows that you have already given similar permission to two other students who had difficulty obtaining needed materials.
- *Situation B.* Martha and Marie are supposed to put the equipment away, but they have left much of it strewn about the gym. Now they are heading for the door in anticipation of the end-of-period bell.
- *Situation C.* Victor has not been working on his assignment. You caught his eye, but he looked away and has continued to talk to nearby students. As you move around the room checking other students' progress, he begins to make a paper airplane.
- *Situation D.* As you walk down the hallway, you hear two students trading insults: "Your mama . . . ," etc. The students are not angry yet, just "fooling around," but several other students are gathering and you think they may encourage the two students to fight.
- *Situation E.* As you begin class, you observe Donalda eating a Twinkie, in violation of the rule prohibiting food in the room. When she sees that you notice her, Donalda stuffs the Twinkie into her mouth and gets another one out of the package.
- *Situation F.* During your current events discussion, Jack and Jill trade notes and laugh inappropriately. You sense that other students' attention is being captured by the duo's antics and you begin to be annoyed by having to compete for class attention.
- *Situation G.* When you were absent yesterday, your fourth-period class gave the substitute teacher a hard time; according to the note he left for you (with a copy sent to the principal!), many students refused to work at all, four or five left for the bathroom and never returned, and a paper-and-spitwad fight raged all period. As the tardy bell rings, you enter the room to greet the fourth-period class.

ASSERTIVENESS ASSESSMENT SCALES

When using the scales on the next page, note that a midrange rating represents an appropriate degree of assertiveness. When rating your own or another teacher's behavior as either nonassertive or hostile, circle the descriptive term that best reflects the basis for your judgment, or write a note on the scale if the descriptors don't adequately capture your perception.

	Unassertive	Assertive	Hostile
	1 _____ 2 _____ 3 _____ 4 _____ 5		
Eye contact	Teacher avoids looking at the student.	Teacher maintains eye contact with student.	Teacher glares at student; stares student down.
	1 _____ 2 _____ 3 _____ 4 _____ 5		
Body language	Teacher turns away, gestures nervously, trembles, fiddles with papers or pen.	Teacher faces student; alert posture but not threatening. Gestures support statements.	Teacher crowds student, points, shakes fist threateningly.
	1 _____ 2 _____ 3 _____ 4 _____ 5		
Message	Obsequious, self-denigrating; excuses student behavior; pleads with student; apologizes.	Clearly states the problem or insists that the behavior stop. Makes own feelings known, may use humor to relieve tension.	Name calling, labeling, blaming, threatening, sarcastic, long lecturing.
	1 _____ 2 _____ 3 _____ 4 _____ 5		
Voice features	Tremulous, whiny, hesitant, broken, or too soft.	Appropriate volume, natural sounding, varied for emphasis.	Too loud; shouts, screams.
	1 _____ 2 _____ 3 _____ 4 _____ 5		
Facial features	Smiles inappropriately; nervous twitches and tics.	Expression suits message.	Excessive affect; contorted, disgusted, enraged expression.

Activity 7-2: Recognizing Listening Responses. Each of the following dialogues depicts a statement and a variety of teacher responses. In each case, decide which one is closest to a listening response, i.e., invites further discussion or best reflects the idea or feeling.

1. *Student:* School sucks.

   a. Don't use that type of language.
   b. You seem upset about school.
   c. Come on, things aren't that bad.
   d. That attitude will get you nowhere.

2. *Student:* I can't understand algebra. Why do we have to learn this stuff?

   a. You'll need it to get into college.
   b. Just keep at it. It'll make sense after a while.
   c. Something isn't making sense to you?
   d. Would you like to come in for extra help after school?

3. *Student:* I don't want to sit near those boys any more.

   a. Sorry, but seats have been assigned for the semester.
   b. If they're bothering you, I can move you.
   c. Can you handle this on your own?
   d. What's the situation?

4. *Parent:* My child is very upset and needs more help or she won't be able to pass. She says she doesn't understand anything.

   a. Please go on. I'd like to hear more about this.
   b. She needs to pay closer attention in class.
   c. She's very anxious but actually she'll do just fine. She only needs to review more before tests.
   d. Most students find my explanations to be quite clear. Perhaps she isn't listening.

5. *Teacher next door:* That fifth period is going to drive me up a wall. They have been impossible lately!

   a. Have you considered being more assertive with them?
   b. I know, everyone in this wing can hear them.
   c. They are really a handful!
   d. You think they're bad, you should have my sixth period.

Activity 7-3: Practicing Empathic Responses. You will need to work with a colleague during this activity. Take turns role playing the student and the teacher. The person role playing the teacher should practice empathic responding skills, and the student should try to behave as naturally as possible. Note that it is assumed that the dialogue is occurring at a time and place that permits this type of interchange and that the teacher is interested in allowing the student to describe the problem. In this exercise, you should avoid giving solutions for the student's problem; instead, concentrate on using listening and processing skills to encourage the student to talk about the situation and think through the problem.

- *Situation A.* Monica is an average student with poor writing skills. With tears in her eyes, she approaches you after class with an essay you have given a failing grade. "I thought that I did okay on this assignment."
- *Situation B.* David, a bright student, offers you some advice: "This class would be a lot more interesting if we didn't have to do all these worksheets. Couldn't we choose our own work sometime?"
- *Situation C.* While the rest of the class is at work on an assignment, Barry closes his book, throws away his assignment sheet, and slinks down in his seat disgustedly.
- *Situation D.* For the second time this week, Sue Ann has not turned in an assignment. Last week she "forgot" to bring her homework twice. After class, you remind Sue Ann that assignments count for half the grade. "I don't care," she responds.
- *Situation E.* Armand, a new student, has been having trouble making friends. Lately he has been getting into arguments with some of the more popular boys, and he has been teasing a few girls, apparently to gain some attention. However, he has not succeeded in breaking into the social scene. After class one day he says to you, "I wish I could transfer back to my old school."

Activity 7-4: Problem-Solving Exercises. Use role playing to practice the problem-solving steps (identify the problem and its consequences, identify and select a solution, obtain a commitment to try it out) with the situations described below. In those situations in which the student is mainly experiencing the problem, assume that the teacher's initial listening response is received positively by the student, so that there is a basis for continuing the discussion and for the teacher to assist the student in thinking through a solution. In cases where the student's behavior is affecting the teacher's ability to teach or interfering with other students' rights, then the student may initially be reluctant to participate in a discussion, and the teacher will need to use assertive skills to overcome this resistance. In addition to the situations listed below, you can also use some of the situations presented in Activities 7-1 and 7-3 for more practice.

- *Situation A.* Bob and Ray are noisy and distracting when they clown around and vie for other students' attention. Reminders and penalties have only fleeting effects on their behavior. Therefore, you decide to have them come in for a conference.

■ *Situation B.* Darnell is good natured as long as no demands are placed upon him. However, when reminded that class time is for learning and for working on assignments, he becomes defiant and insists that it is his right to do whatever he wishes, as long as "I don't hurt no one."

■ *Situation C.* Lucy is a bright student but often turns in work late; frequently it is incomplete. She is able to pass your tests, however, and she could easily be a top student if she were prompt and better organized. Recently you sent her parents a progress report because of missing assignments, and Lucy and her mother have come in for a conference to discuss the situation. As things now stand, Lucy will fail your course this grading period. Her mother wonders whether you will allow Lucy to make up the missing work in order to avoid the failing grade.

CASE STUDY 7-1

WORKING ON A PROBLEM

In the following case study, the teacher uses several of the communication techniques presented in this chapter to deal with a student who is neither particularly cooperative nor especially verbal. The conference takes place in the teacher's classroom at the end of the school day. The teacher had written a referral on the student for frequent violations of class rules, chiefly loud talking with other students, leaving his seat inappropriately, and insubordination. In this school, a referred student must remain in an in-school suspension (ISS) room until the teacher and an assistant principal permit the student to return to class.

Teacher: (*Seated at desk*): Come in and have a seat, Donald. (*Student sits facing teacher.*) I imagine that you know the purpose of our conference?

Student: I guess.

Teacher: Let's be sure we both understand what the situation is. Why don't you tell me what you think happened, and I'll explain my view of it, and we'll see where we stand. Do you want to begin?

Student: Not really.

Teacher: Okay, I'll start. You were referred for doing a lot of loud talking and leaving your seat. We've discussed this before, and you had agreed to do your work and not wander around the room any more. It's also messing up the project activity, and it's keeping me from being able to help other students.

Student: But I wasn't the only one talking. Lots of others were making noise too.

Teacher: It is true that some other students were talking, but they returned to work after a reminder. (*Pauses.*) My problem is that when I have to keep reminding you and watching you, I can't work with other students when I'd like to. What are your thoughts about that?

Student: I don't know.

Teacher: You're not sure what to say?

Student: I guess I could be quiet when you tell me to.

Teacher: That would be helpful, but I recall that you agreed to do that two days ago. Did that work out?

Student: Not very well, but no one's perfect.

Teacher: We all make mistakes. I think it's important to keep trying.

Student: Okay.

Teacher: Do you have any suggestions about what to do to solve this problem.

Student: I should promise to be quiet and then you'll let me out of the ISS room.

Teacher: Not exactly. We need to come up with a plan that will be more specific this time and that has a better chance of working. Remember that the school rule is that if you get another referral the next conference is with your parents, and you get sent to ISS for three days.

Student: Why do they have to get involved in this? It's my business, not theirs.

Teacher: Your parents, you mean? You'd rather settle this on your own, without their involvement.

Student: Right.

Teacher: I can understand that. But it is school policy that after another referral your parents will be called in. So we have to be sure that our agreement will work.

Student: Okay.

Teacher: I'd like to get your ideas about what to do. I don't think anyone is going to make you do anything that you aren't willing to do, and so I think that it will be up to you to agree on what steps need to be taken. Do you have any suggestions?

Student: Well, I like seeing my friends. There's not much time to see them between classes.

Teacher: It's important to have friends and I understand that you want to be with them. But what seems to happen when you do this in class?

Student: I get into trouble.

Teacher: One thing I noticed is that where you are sitting may be a problem, because you are getting distracted by being near some of your buddies. What do you think?

Student: Yeah, I suppose so. They're always talking to me.

Teacher: Donald, would you like to choose another place to sit that would give you a better chance to pay attention to your work instead of to your friends? (*Student nods.*) Look at the seating chart and select a place. I'm going to move a couple of other students around so it won't look like I'm singling you out. (*Student points out another location.*) Okay, that looks like it will work out better than where you are. Now what else can you do to stay out of trouble?

Student: (*Smiles*) I get out of my seat a lot.

Teacher: That's a big one. Any suggestions?

Student: I could just not do it.

Teacher: Okay. But what would help you stop? (*Waits.*) Would it help if the class rule for leaving seats during projects didn't apply to you? In other words, you would be on a different rule. You'll need to stay seated at all times, unless you have permission to be up. That way, you won't have to decide whether to get up or not. I won't announce it to the class, of course—it'll just be between you and me. Would you be willing to try this for one week? Then we'll see if it needs to continue or if we're able to get along without it.

Student: You mean I'll have to stay in my seat all the time?

Teacher: Unless you raise your hand and get permission to leave it.

Student: (*Thinks a few seconds*) Okay, I'll try it.

Teacher: Is this going to be okay with you, or is there something that you think needs to be changed?

Student: No, I think it's okay.

Teacher: I do too. All right Donald, you'll need to write out this plan to show to Mr. Dreadnaught. (*The teacher hands a form to the student.*) Why don't you write out the plan now and I'll sign it so you can turn it in and get back in class tomorrow?

CASE STUDY 7-2

A COOPERATIVE STUDENT WITH A PROBLEM

This short conference occurs at the end of a period with a student who works hard but who has difficulty passing her courses; she is usually cooperative.

Teacher: Serena, I was going over my grade book last night and I noticed that you haven't turned in the last three assignments. What seems to be the problem?

Student: I just didn't get them finished on time, so I didn't turn them in.

Teacher: You started them but you didn't complete them. Why not, Serena?

Student: I just had too many things to do, and I didn't get them done.

Teacher: You were busy with some other work?

Student: Yes, well, no, I mean my mom's looking for another job, so I've got to watch my younger brothers after school and get supper. I just haven't been able to get all my homework done after that.

Teacher: Sounds like you've got an extra load to carry.

Student: I don't mind; it's not that bad.

Teacher: You feel you can handle it at home. What about the schoolwork?

Student: That's a problem, but I'll get at it. My brothers start after-school care next week, so I'll have more time.

Teacher: Sounds like things are looking up. Why don't you turn in whatever you have done on the assignments so you'll get at least partial credit?

Student: Okay. Thanks.

Teacher: See you tomorrow.

Managing
Problem Behaviors

In this chapter we will describe a series of strategies for dealing with problem behaviors that you may encounter as you teach. Although previous chapters have described preventive measures as well as tactics that can be used to manage inappropriate behavior, we think that it will be helpful to consider the full range of approaches that can be used. We hope that you will not encounter problems, especially serious ones, in large numbers. But as you work with adolescents you will undoubtedly face difficult situations that must be dealt with to preserve the climate for learning or to assist a student in developing behaviors more compatible with group life and learning. The aim of this chapter is to pull together and organize a wide array of possible strategies from which you can select. By having a number of approaches to draw upon, you will be better able to choose one that fits specific conditions. Having some alternatives in mind is very useful too, in case your first plan doesn't work.

We hope that this chapter's concern with behavior problems will not be taken as a grim comment on the teacher's role. In particular, the extensive list of strategies in this chapter should be considered within the context of the other chapters in this book. We have advocated generally a positive, supportive climate with major reliance on preventive measures. Within that framework, however, we must be ready to deal with problems when they arise. With a variety of strategies at hand, we can tailor our approach to fit the situation, keeping interruptions to the instructional program to a minimum, and at the same time promoting positive student adjustment and productive behavior.

This chapter's focus is on problem behaviors rather than problem students. Only a small percentage of students exhibit maladaptive behaviors with such consistency and to such a degree that they warrant being labeled emotionally disturbed or behaviorally disordered. Adolescents do, however, behave inappropriately on occasion; we think that it is much more constructive in the long run to deal with the student's behaviors and help the student learn how to behave, rather than impute internal causes for the behavior and assume that the student is restricted in the capacity to make good choices.

On occasion, problem behaviors result from stressors (e.g., abuse, a death in the family, parental unemployment, serious illness, or divorce) the student is experiencing at home or elsewhere. If a student's behavior changes or if inappropriate behavior persists after reasonable attempts to deal with it have been made, then a discussion of the situation with a school counselor, assistant principal, parent, or guardian is in order. Often the student's current or previous teachers can provide additional insights. When you talk with the student about what is happening, use listening skills (see Chapter 7) to try to understand the situation. Be empathic, but help the student understand that acting out (or whatever the problem behavior is) will not help the problem. If you discover that a situation outside the classroom is affecting the student's behavior, discuss what next steps would be appropriate with the student's counselor or assistant principal.

WHAT IS PROBLEM BEHAVIOR?

The concept of problem behavior is very broad. Rather than enumerate all the possible misbehaviors that might occur in classrooms, it is more manageable to think of some categories.

Nonproblem

Brief inattention, some talk during a transition between activities, small periods of woolgathering, and a short pause while working on an assignment are examples of common behaviors that are not really problems for anyone because they are of brief duration and don't interfere with instruction. Everyone is the better for their being ignored. To attempt to react to them would consume too much energy, interrupt lessons constantly, and detract from a positive classroom climate.

Minor Problem

This includes those behaviors that run counter to class procedures or rules but that do not, when occurring infrequently, disrupt class activities nor seriously interfere with student learning. Examples are students calling out or leaving seats without permission, reading or doing unrelated work during class time, passing notes, eating candy, scattering trash around, and excessive social talk during seatwork or group work activities. These behaviors are minor irritants as long as they are brief in duration and are limited to one or a few students; we would not give them much thought except for two reasons. Unattended, they might persist and spread; further, if the behaviors have an audience, then not to respond might cause a perception of inconsistency and potentially undermine an important aspect of the overall management system. Moreover, if students engage in such behavior for an extended period of time, their learning is likely to be adversely affected.

Major Problem, but Limited in Scope and Effects

This category includes behaviors that disrupt an activity or interfere with learning, but whose occurrence is limited to a single student, or perhaps to a few students, but not acting in concert. For example, a student may be chronically off-task. Another student may rarely complete assignments. Or a student may frequently fail to follow class rules for talk or movement around the room or may refuse to do any work. This category also includes a more serious, but isolated, violation of class or school rules; for example, an act of vandalism or cheating on a test.

Escalating or Spreading Problem

In this category we include any minor or major problem that has become commonplace and constitutes a threat to order and to the learning environment. For example, many students roaming around the room at will and continually calling out irrelevant comments make content development activities suffer; social talking that continues unabated even when the teacher repeatedly asks for quiet is distracting to others; and talking back and refusal to cooperate with the teacher is frustrating and may lead quickly to a poor classroom climate. Frequent violations of class guidelines for behavior will cause the management and instructional system to break down and interfere with the momentum of class activities.

GOALS FOR MANAGING PROBLEM BEHAVIOR

Several types of goals need to be considered. We need to judge short-term and long-term effects of any management strategy we choose. In the short term, the desired results are that the inappropriate behaviors cease, and the students resume or begin appropriate behaviors. In the long run, it is important to prevent the problem from recurring. At the same time we must be watchful for potential negative side effects and take steps to minimize them. Effects on the individual student or students causing the problem as well as the effect on the whole class should also be considered.

Joel is talking and showing off to a group of students during seatwork. The teacher could squelch Joel by using a sarcastic put-down or a strong desist, but chooses instead to redirect Joel's behavior and stand close by until he is working on the seatwork assignment. The put-down or strong desist might get quicker results in the short run, but it may lead to resentment or even conflict if Joel tries a rejoinder. Redirection and proximity control take a little more effort, but do not have negative side effects. In addition, they offer more support for appropriate behavior.

The ideal strategy is one that maintains or restores order in the class immediately; in addition, such a strategy would prevent a repetition of the problem and result in the student or students subsequently behaving appropriately in similar situations. In reality, classrooms are very busy places, and we rarely have sufficient time to mull over the various options and their effects whenever a problem arises, especially in the midst of a crisis. If only there were a "pause" button for classroom events! The need for prompt reaction should not, however, deter us from evaluating the results of our efforts and from seeking alternative approaches, especially when our initial efforts do not meet with success. It will, therefore, be useful to have a repertoire of strategies to apply to various problem situations.

MANAGEMENT STRATEGIES

In this section strategies are presented that are useful for dealing with a variety of classroom behavior problems. The first several strategies can be utilized during instruction without much difficulty, require little teacher time, and have the great virtue of being relatively unobtrusive. Thus, they have much to recommend them, because they do not give undue attention to the misbehavior, and they do not interfere with the flow of instructional activity. As we move down the list, we encounter strategies that are more direct attempts to stop the behaviors and to do so quickly; however, the strategies have more negative features: They demand more teacher time, they may have unintended consequences on students, or they interrupt class activities. A general principle that is helpful in selecting a strategy is to use an approach that will be effective in stopping the inappropriate behavior promptly and that has the least negative impact. An implication is that minor problems should usually be dealt with by the use of limited interventions. As problems become more serious, the limited interventions may be ineffective in quickly ending the disruptive behavior and thus a more time-consuming or intrusive intervention may be required.

It should be emphasized that most secondary schools have prescribed procedures to deal with certain types of major problems and sometimes even minor ones. For example, teacher responses to events such as fighting, obscene language, stealing, vandalism, and unexcused absence are likely to be directed by school (or district) policies. Therefore, the beginning teacher must learn what policies are in force and follow them. When no specific policy is established for particular problems or when teachers are given latitude in their response, then the alternatives below will be helpful in guiding teacher action.

It is a given that preventive measures are more desirable than reactive ones. Thus, the contents of earlier chapters have mainly been devoted to establishing a classroom environment that greatly reduces the need for frequent recourse to major interventions. Notwithstanding such efforts, reactive strategies will be needed at times. However, when teachers find themselves frequently using major interventions to deal with problems, it is time to reevaluate the overall management and instructional plan and to make needed modifications. To this end, reviewing suggestions for management presented in prior chapters and perhaps using the checklists to provide focus, could result in changes that would help reduce the problems. Teachers should also be sensitive to the possibility that the source of the problem lies in frustration with content that the student does not grasp or with tasks that the student lacks skills to perform. When the problem is one of a poor fit between student capabilities and academic demands, then the source must also be addressed by developing more appropriate class activities and assignments or by giving the student more assistance.

If you have a special education student whose behavior is causing a problem, then you may find it helpful to discuss the situation with a special education teacher and to ask for suggestions. In particular, ask the teacher if the student has a special discipline program as part of an Individual Education Plan (IEP). Sometimes such a plan will specify particular ways to respond to the student or give some useful alternative strategies. Even if no specific discipline plan is included in the IEP, you may be able to obtain some helpful ideas for working with the student.

We have compiled classroom strategies that have a wide range of application, but the list is certainly not exhaustive. Readers interested in additional sources for ways of coping with specific problems will find a book by Stoner, Shinn, and Walker (1991) helpful. Also, suggestions for managing problems that have reached a crisis level are provided in Pitcher and Poland (1992). Many of the recommendations in the latter book are for school level administrators or school psychologists, but there is much of value for teachers as well.

Minor Interventions

Nonverbal Cues

Make eye contact with the student and give a signal such as a finger to the lips, a head shake (no-no!), or hand signal to issue a desist. Sometimes lightly touching a student on the arm or shoulder will help signal your presence and will have a calming effect.

Get the Activity Moving

Often student behavior deteriorates during transition times between activities or during "dead" time when no apparent focus for attention is present. Students leave their seats, talk, shuffle restlessly, and amuse themselves and each other waiting for something to do. The remedy is obvious: Move through the transition more quickly and reduce or eliminate the dead time. This entails planning activities so that all materials are ready and adhering to a well-conceived lesson plan. Trying to catch and correct inappropriate behaviors during such times is usually futile and misdirected. Just get the next activity underway and cue students to the desired behaviors.

Proximity

Move closer to students. Combine proximity with nonverbal cues to stop inappropriate behavior without interrupting instruction. Be sure to continue monitoring the students at least until they have begun an appropriate activity.

Use Group Focus

Use group alerting, accountability, or a higher participation format (see discussion in Chapter 5) to draw students back into a lesson when attention has begun to wane or when students have been in a passive mode for too long and you observe off-task behavior spreading.

Redirect the Behavior

When students are off-task, remind them of appropriate behavior. "Everyone should be writing answers to the chapter questions," "Be sure that your group is discussing your project plan," "Everyone should be seated and quiet unless you have been given permission to leave your seat or talk." To avoid giving attention to inappropriate behavior, it is best to redirect behavior by stating what should be done. If only one or two students are engaged in inappropriate behavior, a private redirection will be less likely to interrupt the activity or to direct attention toward the incorrect behavior.

Provide Needed Instruction

Especially during seatwork or group work activities, off-task behavior may reflect poor comprehension of the task. Check student work or ask brief questions to assess understanding; give necessary assistance so that students can work independently. If many students can't proceed, stop the activity and provide whole-class instruction. Next time, be sure to check comprehension before starting the independent work activity.

Issue a Brief Desist

Tell the student(s) to stop the undesirable behavior. Make direct eye contact and be assertive (see Chapter 7). Keep your comments brief and then monitor the situation until the student complies. Combine this strategy with redirection in order to encourage desirable behavior.

Give the Student a Choice

Tell the student that he or she has a choice: either to behave appropriately or to continue the problem behavior and receive a consequence. For example, suppose a student has refused to clean up properly after completing a project: "You may choose to clean up now; if not, then you are choosing to stay after class until your area is clean." To a student who continues to distract nearby students: "You may choose to work quietly on your assignment at your seat, or you will need to sit by yourself to do your work." The purpose of stating the consequence as a choice is to emphasize the student's responsibility for his or her behavior. Also, making the consequence clear increases the chance of the student choosing to self-regulate.

Use an "I-message"

An I-message is a statement that describes the problem and its effects on the teacher, the student, or the class; it may also include a description of the feelings produced by the problem. The formula for an I-message is:

- When you (state the problem)

- Then (describe the effect)

- And it makes me feel (state the emotion).

For example, to a student who constantly calls out comments, the teacher might say, "When you talk without permission, it interrupts the lesson, and I get frustrated and resentful." It isn't necessary, of course, to follow the formula exactly; the main idea is to communicate clearly what the problem is and why it's a problem (e.g., "It's very distracting to me and to others when you wander around the room during seatwork.") The I-message can be combined with a brief desist or with redirection. A rationale for using an I-message is that students often act without much awareness of the effects their behavior has on others, and they will change if they realize that they are causing someone a problem. Also, by communicating directly with the student about the effects of the behavior, the teacher implies that the student is capable of controlling the behavior, if only he or she understands its effects.

Moderate Interventions

Strategies in the next set utilize mild punishment (or negative consequences) and act directly to stop the problem behavior. These strategies are more confrontational than the limited interventions described above and thus have greater potential for eliciting resistance. In cases in which the student's behavior has not become especially disruptive, it is desirable to use a minor intervention first or to issue a warning to the student before using these interventions. Doing so will permit the student to exercise self-control and may save teacher time and effort.

Withhold a Privilege or Desired Activity

Students who abuse a privilege (e.g., being allowed to work together on a project, sitting near friends, or freedom to move around the classroom without permission) can lose the privilege and be required to earn it back with appropriate behavior. Sometimes teachers allow quiet talking during seatwork activities, and its removal can be an effective way to limit unproductive behavior. Other teachers allow a class to choose a favorite activity or a short period of free time on one or more days each week as an incentive. Time lost from such activities can then be a strong deterrent to inappropriate behavior at other times. Although withholding a privilege is a form of punishment, it usually has fewer side effects than punishment that requires directly applying an aversive consequence.

Isolate or Remove Students

Students who disrupt an activity can be removed to some other area of the room, away from other students. It is helpful to have a carrel with sides or at least a desk at the back of the room facing away from other students to discourage eye contact from the time-out area. If no suitable place is available, then the student may need to have time out in the hall outside the door, although not if your school has a policy prohibiting this because of the problem of adequately supervising the student.

Time out is a variation on the preceding consequence, in that it takes away the student's privilege of participating in the classroom activity. It is a good idea to allow excluded students to return to the activity in a short time, as long as their behavior in time out is acceptable. Some teachers prefer to let the student retain some control over the return, using a direction such as, "You may come back to the activity in five minutes if you decide that you can follow our class rules." Other teachers prohibit the student from returning until the activity is completed or until they have a brief conference with the student.

A problem with time out is that some students may find it rewarding. They receive attention when it is administered, and it allows them to avoid an activity they dislike. When this occurs, you should switch to another strategy. Another problem is that a student may refuse to go to the time-out area. Usually this is a temporary problem; if you are firm, ignoring the student's protests and continuing with the activity, the student will go eventually. One way to move a recalcitrant body is to offer a choice: "You can either take time out or you can take a walk to the principal's office. It's your decision."

Time out has another risk. Its use clearly identifies a student as someone who is excludable, and it may result in implicit labeling by the teacher, by other students, or by the excluded student. If used frequently with an individual student, it may cause resentment and anger. Therefore, be sure to provide opportunities for the student to resume full participation in the class, and use other strategies to promote appropriate behavior at the same time.

Use a Fine or Penalty

Sometimes a small amount of repetitive work is required as payment for inappropriate behavior. For example, in physical education, students may be required to run an extra lap or do some push-ups. In math, students may have to write multiplication tables or work some extra problems. In a language class, students can write verb conjugations. The advantage of this type of consequence is that it can usually be administered quickly with a minimum of teacher time and effort. A disadvantage is that the task is being defined as punishing, and therefore the student's attitude toward the content may be negatively affected. Another problem with the use of fines or penalties is that their ease of use can lead to overuse, detracting from the overall climate.

Assign Detention

Another penalty that is commonly used is to require that the student serve a detention, either at lunch, or before or after school. Because of the logical relation between the problem and the consequence, this penalty is often used for misbehaviors that involve time (e.g., tardiness, extended goofing off and time-wasting; behavior that interferes with instruction or student work time). Other common uses of the penalty are for repeated rule violations and for frequent failure to complete assignments. You may need to supervise the detention in your room, or your school might have a D-Hall with an assigned monitor. The time in detention need not be lengthy, especially for misbehaviors that are not severe or frequent; a ten- or fifteen-minute detention is often sufficient to make the point.

An advantage of detention as a penalty is that it is disliked by most students and they want to avoid it; at the same time, it is administered away from other students in the class and thus does not give undue attention to the behavior. Also, it is a common punishment, so extensive explanations and unusual procedures aren't needed. Finally, the teacher can sometimes use a little of the detention time to hold a conference with the student and perhaps work out a plan for improving the situation.

A disadvantage of detention is that it does take teacher time, especially when the teacher must supervise it. Even when the school has a D-Hall, the teacher still will need to write a referral. Another disadvantage is that students might be able to avoid detention, at least in the short run, simply by not showing up. Thus, the teacher or the school must have a backup plan, such as doubling the time; moreover, records must be kept and often additional time will be required to deal with such students.

Use a School-Based Consequence

If your school has a prescribed consequence for particular problem behaviors and you are allowed some latitude in its administration, you should consider utilizing it after you have not had desired results with other strategies. For example, some schools have a system of referral to an assistant principal, who then deals with the student. Often, a first referral consequence is limited to detention or to a warning, with subsequent referrals resulting in a parent conference. It is necessary to apprise the administrator of the basis for the referral and, if time permits, to discuss what outcome is desirable. Advantages of this approach are that it does not require much teacher time and it is often an effective limit for students who do not respond to other consequences. A disadvantage is that the usefulness of this strategy is dependent on others for its effectiveness; also, extensive and frequent external support for handling in-class problems is not a realistic option in most schools.

More Extensive Interventions

When students do not respond to minor or moderate interventions and their behavior continues to disrupt classroom activities and to interfere with their own and others' learning, one or more of the strategies described below can be helpful in reducing the inappropriate behaviors and allowing the teacher to reestablish a focus on learning.

Individual Contract with the Student

When a student's inappropriate behavior has become chronic or if a problem is severe and must stop immediately, try an individual contract. You will need to discuss the nature of the problem with the student, including the student's perspective on it. Then you and the student can identify appropriate solutions and agree on which course of action to take. Typically, the contract specifies changes the student will make, but it might also call for the teacher to alter some behavior or activity. You should also make clear what consequences will occur if the plan is not followed, and you can also identify some incentive to encourage the student to follow through with the contract. The plan and consequences are written down and signed by the student. Contracts can also be used with other strategies (see the Five-Step Plan and the Reality Therapy sections below).

Conference with a Parent

Sometimes a telephone call to a parent can have a marked effect on a student's behavior, signaling to the student that accountability for behavior extends beyond the classroom. Parents react best if they don't feel that they are being held responsible for their child's behavior in school (after all, they aren't there), so don't put the parent on the defensive. Describe the situation briefly and say that you would appreciate whatever support the parent can give in helping you understand and resolve the problem. Acknowledge the difficulty of rearing adolescents as well as teaching them. Be sure to use listening skills (see Chapter 7) during the conversation, and be alert for information that might help you determine an appropriate strategy for dealing with the student. Have your grade book handy so that you can give the parent specific information about the student's progress, if the information is requested or needed.

Rather than a phone conference, you might need to schedule a face-to-face conference with a parent. Sometimes, but by no means always, when such conferences are arranged it is because a problem has become quite severe, and other school personnel (e.g., a counselor or principal) may need to be present. If you have initiated the meeting, you should try to brief the others and plan your approach ahead of time.

The chief drawback to parent conferences is the time and energy they require. The effort is frequently worth it; although not every conference is successful, many times the student's behavior will improve. Another potential problem is identifying ahead of time what strategy would be best to follow with the parent. Occasionally parents overreact and punish children excessively. As the year progresses, you will get to know parents better and be able to gauge the probable effects of your call or conference.

Use a Check or a Demerit System

This approach is used with the entire class; it requires the teacher to give a check or demerit when a student violates some rule or rules. If a student persists in the misbehavior, then additional checks are given. A specific penalty is attached to receiving one or more checks, for example, fifteen minutes of detention. An example of this approach is the "name-on-the-board" system suggested by Canter and Canter (1976, 1989). The teacher provides a list of rules to the students and informs them of the consequences of violations. A typical plan would be for the teacher to write the student's name on the board after the first violation, put a check mark after the second infraction, and so on. Associated consequences would be a warning for the name-on-the-board, followed by fifteen minutes detention after each check. More severe penalties are added after the third check (e.g., call the parents or send the student to the principal). The student starts with a clean slate each day. More recently, Canter has suggested using a clipboard instead of the chalkboard to record student names. A clipboard avoids the public display of student names and thus reduces the risk of giving them undue attention. It also preserves a record of problem behaviors and perhaps makes follow-up more effective.

A variation on this procedure is a demerit system in which rule violations (e.g., tardiness, failure to bring text or other materials, excessive talking) are recorded on a form which the teacher retains in a file folder for each class. In this approach, a record is maintained by the teacher and the student is required to sign the form acknowledging responsibility for the behavior. Consequences initially are mild, but after several infractions in a given period of time, detention, a parent conference, or a behavior contract might be used. Students can be allowed to erase demerits with good behavior; e.g., no rule violations for a week.

An advantage of these systems is that they can help teachers set and maintain limits consistently. In addition, they make the consequences of rule violations clear to students and thus increase the predictability of the classroom environment. There are, however, several potential disadvantages. Probably the chief problem is the emphasis on catching students being bad. Whether the student's name goes on the chalkboard, clipboard, or on a piece of paper, attention is directed at the misbehavior. This may not be a major drawback if checks or demerits aren't given frequently and if the teacher is careful also to give students positive attention. If, however, many checks or demerits are given, then not only are misbehaviors receiving attention, but the flow of the lesson will be impeded, compounding the classroom management problems. Finally, if the inappropriate behaviors are not easy to observe accurately, then it will be very difficult to appear consistent in the use of these systems. For example, trying to manage side talk during seatwork would be impossible in many classrooms, because it is too hard to detect each time it occurs.

Teachers sometimes adopt the name-on-the-board strategy as a last resort when student misbehaviors have become frequent and they believe they are in danger of losing control of a class. Unfortunately, this is the situation in which this type of consequence system is most likely to break down, because the teacher spends excessive time attending to inappropriate behavior and to punishing students. If a class has become unruly, we suggest choosing one activity (e.g., seatwork or content development) and targeting for this system only one or two easily observable but problematic behaviors (e.g., being out of seat without permission, continuing to talk after being asked by the teacher to stop). Students should know exactly what behaviors are not allowed and also what behaviors are desired. To avoid the teacher's having to play the role of "sheriff" all the time, the system should be used only in that specific activity (i.e., not for the entire period). The activity should be kept short and briskly paced during the first several days of implementation to increase the chances of success. Attention should also be provided for appropriate behaviors and appreciation should be communicated for students' greater maturity and improved behavior. When student behavior is under reasonable control in the selected activity, the system can be used in another activity if necessary.

Use Problem Solving

Because problem solving was described extensively in Chapter 7, it will not be discussed in this chapter. However, the next two strategies, which share some features with problem solving, are sufficiently unique to warrant a separate presentation.

Use a Five-step Intervention Procedure

Jones and Jones (1990) recommend following five steps (Figure 8-1) when dealing with disruptive student behavior.

Step 1: Use a nonverbal signal to cue the student to stop.

Step 2: If the behavior does not cease, then ask the student to follow the desired rule.

Step 3: If the disruption continues, give the student a choice of stopping the behavior or choosing to develop a plan.

Step 4: If the student still does not stop, then require that the student move to a designated area in the room to write a plan.

Step 5: If the student refuses to comply with Step 4, then send the student to another location (e.g., the school office) to complete the plan.

The use of the five-step intervention process requires a form for the plan (Figure 8-2). When the approach is introduced to the students, preferably at the beginning of the year, the teacher explains its purpose and how to fill out the form. Role playing the use of the five steps is recommended, both to teach the procedures as well as to provide a positive model of their application. It will also

FIGURE 8-1 Steps in Responding to Students' Violation of Rules and Procedures

Step	Procedure	Example
1.	Nonverbal cue	Raised index finger
2.	Verbal cue	"John, please follow our classroom rules."
3.	Indicate choice student is making	"John, if you continue to talk while I am talking, you will be choosing to develop a plan."
4.	Student moves to a designated area in the room to develop a plan	"John, you have chosen to take time to develop a plan."
5.	Student is required to go somewhere else to develop a plan.	"John, because you are choosing not to be responsible, you will need to see Mrs. Johnson to develop your plan."

From Vernon F. Jones and Louise S. Jones, COMPREHENSIVE CLASSROOM MANAGEMENT: MOTIVATING AND MANAGING STUDENTS, Third Edition. Copyright © 1990 by Allyn and Bacon. Reprinted with permission.

be helpful to laminate a couple of examples of appropriate plans so that students have models.

Advantages of this approach include its emphasis on student responsibility and choice. Also, a graduated response to the problem allows the teacher to intervene nonpunitively at first, and thus provides a means of settling the matter quickly with a minimum of disturbance to the on-going activity. The steps are simple and straightforward, which will promote consistency in their use by the

FIGURE 8-2. Problem-Solving Form

CHOOSE TO BE RESPONSIBLE

Name _____ Date _____

Rules we agreed on

1. Speak politely to others
2. Treat each other kindly
3. Follow teacher requests
4. Be prepared for class
5. Make a good effort at your work and request help if you need it
6. Obey all school rules

Please answer the following questions:

1. What rule did you violate? _____
   _____

2. What did you do that violated this rule? _____
   _____

3. What problem did this cause for you, your teacher, or classmates?_____
   _____

4. What plan can you develop that will help you be more responsible and follow this classroom rule? _____
   _____

5. How can the teacher or other students help you? _____
   _____

I, _____ , will try my best to follow the plan I have written and to follow all the other rules and procedures in our classroom that we created to make the classroom a good place to learn.

---

teacher; students, in turn, will be aided by the structure and predictability of the approach.

A disadvantage of the system is that movement from Step 1 to Step 5 can occur very rapidly and some intermediate strategies may be necessary in order to avoid excessive reliance on sending students out. In addition, some students will have difficulty writing an acceptable plan by themselves. Finally, setting up the system and, later, meeting with students to discuss their plans and monitoring implementation require at least a moderate investment of time.

Use the Reality Therapy Model

William Glasser's (1976, 1977) ideas have been widely applied in education. Some of his recommendations for dealing with disruptive or maladaptive behaviors in a classroom setting are presented below.

The essential features of using a Reality Therapy strategy when working with an individual student include establishing a caring relationship with the student, focusing on the present behaviors, getting the student to accept responsibility, developing a plan for change, obtaining a commitment to follow the plan, and following up. Glasser believes strongly that students choose behavior depending on their perceptions of its consequences. Most students will choose appropriate behaviors when they believe these will lead to desirable outcomes and they will avoid behaviors that they perceive will lead to undesirable consequences. Glasser's plan can be put into effect by following the steps below.

Step 1: Establish involvement with the students. If students believe that the teacher cares for them and has their best interests in mind, then they will be more likely to follow the teacher's guidance when evaluating and changing their behavior. Teachers can show commitment to and caring for students in numerous ways: commenting favorably to the students about their work; being friendly; and showing an interest in different students' activities, family, likes and dislikes, and hobbies. Teachers can also get involved by demonstrating school spirit, joking, being a good listener, and taking time to talk with students about their concerns. The best time to establish involvement is before a student becomes disruptive, but even if a student has begun to exhibit problem behavior, it is not too late to begin. When a teacher makes a special effort just to have two or three friendly contacts a day with such a student, it can be helpful in creating a more positive climate for change.

Step 2: Focus on behavior. When a problem has occurred, Glasser recommends that a brief conference be held with the student. The initial concern should be to determine what the problem is. To this end, the teacher should ask only questions about "what happened" or "what's going on" and avoid trying to fix blame. Even if the teacher knows exactly what the problem is, it is wise to obtain the student's perspective.

Step 3: The student needs to accept responsibility for the behavior. This means that the student acknowledges that he or she did engage in the behavior. No excuses are accepted. For the student to admit responsibility is difficult, especially when there are so many other handy things to blame. Of course, it is possible that more than one individual is responsible for the problem, but that should not be an excuse for irresponsibility or denial.

Step 4: The student should evaluate the behavior. If students have difficulty perceiving their part or they minimize it, Glasser suggests asking, "Has the behavior helped or hurt you? Has it helped or hurt others?" The teacher may need to point out the negative consequences of continuing the behavior. Unless the student sees that it will lead to negative consequences and that changing it will produce desirable consequences, there isn't much reason to expect a change.

Step 5: Develop a plan. The teacher and student need to identify ways to prevent the problem from recurring, and what new behaviors are needed. The plan can be written as a contract.

Step 6: The student must make a commitment to follow the plan. Progress will be limited at best if students do not seriously intend to make a change. It may help if the teacher makes clear the positive and negative consequences of following or not following the plan. The plan needs to be do-able in a reasonable time.

Step 7: Follow-up and follow through. If the plan doesn't work, it should be modified with the student; if a negative consequence was called for in the plan it should be used. Glasser also proposes several additional steps beyond the classroom if a student continues to be a problem. For example, use of in-school suspension could be a consequence of continuing misbehavior; before the student is allowed to return to the classroom, an acceptable plan would need to be agreed upon. Only after several attempts to obtain a change have failed should the teacher refer the student to the principal.

The Reality Therapy approach to dealing with individual discipline problems has much to recommend it. It is a systematic way for teachers to deal with many kinds of individual student problems, and it provides a simple, yet effective, process for getting right at the issues, and avoiding being sidetracked by fault finding, conning, or excuse making. Research on the effects of this aspect of Reality Therapy is generally supportive (Emmer and Aussiker, 1990) for applications to individual students.

SPECIAL PROBLEMS

In addition to the general types of problems described at the beginning of this chapter, some specific types occur commonly enough and are severe enough that it will be worthwhile to describe additional strategies for managing them. Previously described approaches can also be applied to these behaviors.

Rudeness Toward the Teacher

This may take the form of sassy back talk, arguing, crude remarks, or gesturing. An important consideration with this type of behavior is not to overreact or argue with the student. Frequently the behavior is a means of getting attention either from you or from peers, so don't get trapped into a power struggle. Your response will depend to some extent on the degree of rudeness. In borderline cases the student may not even realize that a comment was offensive. A reasonable first reaction is to inform the student that the behavior is not acceptable and to refer to a general classroom rule such as "Respect others" or "Be polite." If the incident is repeated, or if the original comment was quite rude, then some type of penalty can be used. In the case of really obnoxious behavior that disrupts the class or that persists, the student can be sent to the school office and not allowed to return until he or she agrees to behave appropriately. Usually the school will have a standard policy for dealing with extreme cases, and you should use whatever procedures have been established.

Chronic Avoidance of Work

You may have students who frequently do not complete assigned work. Sometimes they fail to complete assignments early in the school year; more often a student will begin to skip assignments occasionally and then with increasing regularity, until he or she is habitually failing to do the work. This behavior can be minimized by an accountability system that clearly ties student work to grades (review Chapter 3 for details). However, even in classrooms with a strong accountability system, some students still may avoid work.

It is much easier (and much better for the student) if you deal with this problem before the student gets so far behind that failure is almost certain. By catching the problem early, you will still be able to provide some incentive (that is, passing the course) for the student to get back on track. In order to be in a position to take early action, you must collect and check student work frequently and also maintain good records. Then, when you note a student who has begun to miss assignments, you can talk with him or her to identify the problem. It is possible that the student is simply unable to do the work. If so, then you may be able to arrange appropriate assistance or modify the assignments for that student.

It is also possible that the student feels overwhelmed by the assignments. In this case break up the assignments into parts, whenever possible. Have the student complete the first part of the assignment within a specified period of time (for example, five or ten minutes), then check to see that it has been done. A bonus of a few minutes of free time at the end of the period (for example, to sit quietly, read, do an enrichment activity, or help with a classroom chore) can be offered for completion of the portion within the time limit or for working steadily without prodding.

If ability is not the problem, then in addition to talking with the student, the following procedures can be used. Call the student's parents or guardian and discuss the situation. Often the home can supply the extra support needed to help motivate the student. Also, if the student participates in athletics or other extracurricular activities, the coaches or other supervising faculty may be able to support your efforts. Many schools have a system (for example, a weekly checklist) for monitoring academic progress of students involved in certain extracurricular activities. Finally, apply the consequence, usually a failing grade, for repeated neglect of work. There is no purpose served in softening the penalty because the student promises to do the work during the next grading period or because you think that he or she could do better by just working harder. Doing so teaches the student to avoid responsibility.

Fighting

This is rarely a classroom problem; usually it occurs in hallways or in other areas of the school. Whether or not to intervene directly will depend on your judgment as to whether you can do so without undue risk of injury. If you do not intervene directly, you should of course alert other teachers and administrators so that action can be taken. If you do intervene, try to do so with the assistance of one or several adults. It is hard to stop a fight by yourself, particularly when a crowd has gathered. Your school will undoubtedly have a procedure to deal with fighting, so you should familiarize yourself with your responsibility (for example, to file a report with the office). Typically, students will be questioned by an assistant principal who will call the student's home, arrange a conference, and mete out any prescribed penalty, such as suspension.

Other Aggressive Behavior

Students engage in other types of aggressive behavior toward fellow students besides fighting, and it may occur in the classroom. Examples include name calling, overbearing bossiness or rudeness toward other students, and physically aggressive—but "playful"—pushing, shoving, or slapping. Offending students should be told that such behavior is not acceptable, even if it is just "fooling

"... and suddenly there were teachers
all over the place!"

around." It can easily escalate. Refer to whatever class rule fits the situation, such as "Respect others." Give no more than one warning and then assess an appropriate penalty. Students engaged in such behavior should be separated and seated apart if they give any indication of intending to persist.

Defiance or Hostility Toward the Teacher

This type of behavior is understandably very threatening, particularly when it occurs in front of other students. The teacher feels, and rightfully so, that if the student is allowed to get away with it, such behavior may continue, and other students will be more likely to react this way. The student, however, has provoked the confrontation, usually publicly, and backing down would cause a loss of face in front of peers. The best way to deal with such an event is to try to defuse it. This can be done by keeping it private and handling it individually with the student, if possible. If it occurs during a lesson and is not really extreme, deal with it by trying to depersonalize the event and avoid a power struggle. "This is taking time away from the lesson. I will discuss it with you in a few minutes when I have time." Then leave the student alone and give him or her a chance to calm down. Later, when you have time, have a private talk with the student and assess a penalty if it seems warranted. Should the student not accept the opportunity you have provided but rather press the confrontation further, you can instruct the student to leave the room and wait in the hall. After the student has had time to cool off, you can give your class something to do and discuss the problem privately with the student.

When presented with this type of behavior, you should try to stay objective. Don't engage in arguments with the student. Point out that the behavior was not acceptable and state the penalty clearly. Listen to the student's point of view, and if you are not sure how to respond, say that you will think about it and discuss it later.

In an extreme (and rare) case, the student may be totally uncooperative and refuse to keep quiet or to leave the room. If this happens, you can send another student to the office for assistance. In almost all cases, however, as long as you stay calm and refuse to get into a power struggle with the student, the student will take the opportunity to cool down.

A Final Reminder: Think and Act Positively

In this chapter, many of the strategies for dealing with problem behaviors involve some form of punishment. This is especially the case for the strategies in the moderate and extensive categories. A drawback to punishment is that, by itself, it doesn't teach students what behaviors should be practiced. Consequently, it is important also to communicate clearly what behaviors are desired. That is, the focus should remain on teaching appropriate behaviors. Furthermore, a classroom in which the main consequences are negative will not have a very good climate. Thus, teachers using strategies in the moderate and extensive categories more than occasionally may wish to incorporate some additional incentives or a reward system into their overall classroom management to help mitigate the effects of using punishment. Finally, after correcting student behavior, the teacher who supplies a generous measure of warmth and support will reassure students that they have been restored to good grace.

SUGGESTED ACTIVITIES

1. Review the descriptions of problem types presented at the beginning of the chapter. Then decide which interventions would be best suited for each type. Given several alternative interventions for any type of problem, how would you decide which to use?

2. Within each type of intervention—minor, moderate, or extensive—are there any that you distinctly prefer? Do you reject any? Discuss your reasons for liking or disliking particular approaches.

3. Listed below are several problem behaviors. Decide on a strategy for dealing with each, and also an alternative response if your first approach does not produce good results. Indicate any assumptions you are making about the teaching context as you choose your strategy.

- *Situation 1.* Ardyth and Melissa talk and pass notes as you conduct a class discussion. Several other students whisper or daydream.

- *Situation 2.* Desi and Bryce talk constantly. They refuse to get to work and argue with you when you ask them to open their books.

- *Situation 3.* Joe manages to get most of his work done, but in the process he is constantly disruptive. He teases the girls sitting around him, keeping them constantly laughing and competing for his attention. Joe makes wisecracks in response to almost anything you say. When confronted, he grins charmingly and responds with exaggerated courtesy, much to the delight of the rest of the class.

- *Situation 4.* When someone bumped into Marc at the drinking fountain, he turned around and spit water at the other student. Later, Marc ordered a boy who was standing near his desk to get away, and he then shoved the boy. On the way back from the cafeteria, Marc got into a name-calling contest with another boy.

- *Situation 5.* Behavior in your third period class has been deteriorating. Class discussions are interrupted by irrelevant comments and an undercurrent of talking makes it difficult to conduct activities. Students write notes as you teach, talk during seatwork assignments, and complain about having to do any work. Many students do no work during the last 10 minutes of the period as they get ready to leave and spend the time chatting.

Managing Special Groups

Although the management principles and guidelines discussed in previous chapters generalize to most classroom settings, classroom management is, of course, affected by the characteristics of the students making up a class. The ages, academic ability levels, goals, interests, and home backgrounds of students have an impact on their classroom behavior. Consequently, effective teachers adjust their managerial and instructional practices to meet the needs of different groups of students. Two groups that frequently present some special challenges are very heterogeneous classes and low ability or remedial level classes.

Among the groups that frequently present some special challenges are students who are working substantially below or well above grade level, students who are academically or physically handicapped, and students whose English language skills are limited. Often a classroom includes several of these types of students, presenting a particular challenge to a teacher's managerial skills. Accommodating such diverse needs and abilities requires extra effort. This chapter presents information and suggestions that, combined with the principles in previous chapters, will help you organize and manage classes with a range of student achievement or ability levels, groups of students with below level skills, and students with special needs.

TEACHING HETEROGENEOUS CLASSES

Many secondary school classrooms contain students with a very wide range of entering achievement levels. For example, a very heterogeneous eighth-grade English class may include some students who score at fourth-grade levels on reading and language usage achievement tests and other students with grade-equivalent scores of eleventh grade or higher. In junior high mathematics classes, students' entering achievement levels may be spread across five or more grade levels. Required science and social studies courses often present extremes of student heterogeneity, with students' entering achievement levels in reading comprehension, mathematical reasoning, and content knowledge varying greatly. Of course, any class is to some extent heterogeneous: No two students are alike. Ideally, every individual student should receive instruction tailored to his or her needs, abilities, interests, and learning style. In practice, the pupil/teacher ratio in most secondary schools makes large group instruction the most common and efficient means of teaching the standard curriculum. However, in very heterogeneous classes a whole-class assignment may be unchallenging or repetitious for some students and too difficult for the very low achievers. Students who are bored or frustrated are not likely to stay involved in activities, and inappropriate or disruptive behavior may result. Extreme heterogeneity may, therefore, have an impact on the management of student behavior as well as on instruction. Attempting to cope with heterogeneity by using many different assignments, providing an individualized, self-paced program, or using small group instruction extensively in secondary classrooms increases the complexity of classroom management, requires a great deal of planning and preparation, and may require instructional materials that are not readily available. Rather than completely altering their instructional approach, many effective teachers provide for different levels of student ability by supplementing their whole-class instruction with limited use of special materials, activities, assignments, and small group work. The following instructional procedures will help you cope successfully with very heterogeneous classes.

Assessing Entering Achievement

The first step in planning for instruction in a heterogeneous class is to gather information about students' entering achievement levels and skills in areas that will affect their ability to succeed in your classroom. You can get this information by investigating existing test scores, administering pretests, and carefully assessing student performance on classwork in the first weeks of school. Results of achievement or aptitude testing from the previous school year may be available through the counselors' office. Examining these scores will give you an idea of the extent of differences in your classes and will identify outlying students. Of course, achievement test scores are less than perfect indicators, and scores may not be available for all your students, so you will probably want to consider existing test data in conjunction with your own pretests or informal assessments. To select an appropriate pretest, consult with the department chairperson, with other teachers in your academic department, or with the curriculum coordinator or supervisor in your district. The teacher's edition of your textbook may include a recommended pretest. If a prepared test is not available, you will have to prepare your own, based on content from the first part of the textbook your students will use.

You can also obtain useful information about student ability levels in your classes by carefully examining students' classwork at the beginning of the year. For example, in many courses the ability to follow a lecture and take good notes is important. It is a good idea, therefore, to present a short typical lecture at the beginning of the year, telling students ahead of time that you will be collecting and checking their notes. This assessment will help you identify students who are likely to need special assistance and monitoring during content development activities. Similarly, requiring that students read a short section of the text, outline it, and answer some comprehension questions in class will give you an idea of the range of students' abilities to learn from the textbook you will be using.

Information on student needs and other characteristics, such as student interests and backgrounds, can also affect learning and instruction and should be considered whenever possible as you plan instructional activities and set goals. For instance, such information can be used to plan extra-credit projects and alternative assignments, as well as to identify small groups for instruction, to pair students for peer tutoring, or to create cooperative groups for learning activities.

Modifying Whole-Group Instruction

Once you have information about how heterogeneous your classes are, you can plan appropriate adjustments of your instruction. First, consider ways that you can accommodate different student needs simply by modifying your whole-class activities.

Participation

During class discussions, recitations, or content development activities, be careful to include all students. Use some system (for example, write each students' name on a 3-by-5 card, shuffle, and then systematically go through the stack) to be sure each student has opportunities to participate frequently. Guard against the tendency to focus only on the higher (or lower) achieving students, allowing them to set the pace for the lesson.

Accountability Procedures

In very heterogeneous classes carefully planned and implemented student accountability procedures become especially important. You need to get information daily about how all students are performing, and students will benefit from frequent individual feedback. Your accountability system should accommodate extra-credit or enrichment assignments, and it must also be designed so that lower achieving students who work diligently and make progress can make a satisfactory grade.

Seating Arrangement

If you have one or two students who are especially likely to have trouble with whole-class assignments, place these students where you can easily keep an eye on them during instruction and seatwork. As soon as you have given seatwork instructions to the whole class and have monitored to ensure that students have begun work, check with the slower student(s) privately, either to go over instructions again or to modify the assignment, as needed. If there are more than two such students it may be more efficient to treat them as a small group when giving supplemental instructions.

Flexible Assignments

Include some classroom activities that can be done together as a whole class but at different levels by different students. Use a grading or credit system that emphasizes individual student progress rather than competition among students. Examples of such activities include projects or reports, reading assignments of varying difficulty, and fluency writing exercises in which students write for a specified period of time on an assigned topic, trying to increase the number of words they can generate each day. Other assignments that can be challenging to students at many different achievement levels include various composition and creative thinking assignments with open-ended directions such as: List all the Spanish -ar verbs you can think of; name as many protein foods (or mammals, or words with EAT in them, or nations, and so on) as you can. When assigning research papers or projects, provide some choice of topics, or assign topics to students individually, adjusting the difficulty of the topic and the amount of structure you provide according to student ability.

Supplementary Materials

Supplement whole-group instruction by providing enrichment materials for high achieving students and remedial (review or practice) materials for lower achieving students. These materials can be used as the basis for regular, differentiated assignments or as extra-credit options. To differentiate class or homework assignments, plan a core or basic assignment that all students must complete. Then provide an additional part or parts that are either optional (for example, for those seeking an A grade) or required of different groups (for example, different spelling groups). Begin building a collection of supplementary materials by examining workbooks and texts from other grade levels, borrowing from other teachers and your curriculum coordinator, and reading from professional journals and magazines in your content area. Do not assign work from the next year's official textbooks, however, since that would deprive the teacher of basic content material.

Enrichment or extra-credit material for students who finish classwork early should be work related and should not distract other students. Avoid free-time activities that are so attractive that slower working students feel deprived or are tempted to stop or rush through their work. Provide supplementary reading materials at a variety of reading levels. Set up a system for giving credit, feedback, or recognition for completion of enrichment activities.

Peer Tutoring

Peer tutoring provides an opportunity for one or more students to receive one-on-one assistance, particularly when the teacher is unavailable to provide assistance. This can be done during class by pairing students at similar levels to work together or by asking a student who has achieved a certain level or learned a concept to work with another student who has not. The student who receives assistance benefits from individualized instruction. The helper, or peer tutor, benefits from planning for and providing instruction.

To use peer tutoring effectively, certain management issues must be addressed. You must decide when tutoring is and is not acceptable. There may be some topics for which peer tutoring is not appropriate. For instance, you may not be assured that the potential peer tutors have sufficiently learned the concept to be able to provide assistance.

You will also want to decide where tutoring will occur. Some teachers provide a special location within the classroom where peer interactions are less likely to interrupt other classroom activities or disturb students who are working unassisted. Others may allow students to work quietly side-by-side at their desks.

If you are going to use peer tutors frequently, it is a good idea to discuss with them the behaviors their role will require. Potential peer tutors should be shown how to model desired behaviors (e.g., demonstrate a skill or explain a concept), instructed in how to ask questions to assess the other student's understanding, and counseled on interpersonal behaviors. For long-term peer tutors, you may be able to provide brief training during class or before or after school. Other directions can be given as part of the overall instructions for an activity.

Cooperative Work Groups

For many activities, using small work groups or learning teams with mixed-ability levels and/or diverse backgrounds provides a good opportunity for all students to help and to learn from each other. Often such groups are used as an alternative to individual seat work after the teacher has provided whole-class instruction. Sometimes groups are used very extensively to organize instructional activities in a class. Researchers such as Robert Slavin (1990) have shown that working in mixed-ability teams can benefit both higher and lower achieving students in many subject areas. Benefits of cooperative groups can include increased student achievement, positive race relations, and increased student self-esteem. Not all researchers or educators agree that learning teams are as effective as their proponents have argued. However, we believe the evidence indicates that they are an important approach for dealing with heterogeneous groups.

Effective use of cooperative student groups requires several components: mixed-ability (or background) groups, a reward structure that provides for individual accountability as well as group rewards, and academic tasks that lend themselves to completion in a group format.

The selection of appropriate cooperative groups entails careful assigning of students to groups or teams rather than just letting students choose to work with their friends and designating student roles within the groups to ensure that all students play an active part. Most cooperative work group designs call for a mixture of high achieving (or high ability), average achieving, and lower achieving students or students with special needs. In some types of cooperative group activities, each student is expected to take responsibility for a certain amount of lesson content, to instruct the rest of the group in that content, and to learn from other group members the content for which they are responsible. In other types of cooperative group activities the students work together to complete a task and to ensure that all group members have learned the content. Each member of the group is expected to participate.

An essential component of cooperative groups is the reward/accountability structure. An effective reward structure includes a combination of individual and group rewards. Each individual in the group must feel that his or her performance will be evaluated individually for effort and accomplishment. In addition, rewarding the group's performance encourages the interaction of group members working toward a common purpose.

The use of cooperative groups entails a number of management considerations. Determining what behaviors are needed and then translating these expectations into a clear set of procedures and routines will be important. Areas for concern will include volume and nature of student talk, arrangement of the physical space, movement around the room, access to materials, and how to obtain assistance. Procedures for monitoring group progress without hovering should also be planned. It will be important to determine the extent of prior experience your students have had with cooperative groups. Also, how you introduce the learning group process and train students to be good group participants is an important part of using this instructional strategy successfully. More detailed treatment of cooperative groups is beyond the scope of this book, so if you decide to use them, we suggest that you do some reading on the topic. Books by Johnson and Johnson (1987) and by Slavin (1991) would be good possibilities. Also, try to talk with and observe a teacher who uses the technique. Even better, attend an inservice workshop or college class on the topic.

Small-Group Instruction

In some classes or in some content areas, the preceding suggestions for modifying or supplementing whole-class instruction may not be adequate to solve the heterogeneity problem. In these classes teachers might need to use small group instruction, forming relatively homogeneous subgroups. This commonly occurs in reading courses, in English classes for spelling instruction, or in mathematics classes where some students lack skills in basic operations necessary to go on to more advanced work. In many subjects small-group instruction might be used as a temporary measure with a group of students who have failed to pass a criterion-referenced test covering material that is prerequisite to subsequent units. The following are some examples of how small-group instruction might be conducted in secondary classes.

An eighth-grade English teacher uses small-group instruction for spelling only. She has three groups: six students using spelling materials at the fourth-grade level, sixteen at the eighth-grade level, and five using advanced materials to prepare them for interscholastic competition. After opening class the teacher goes over general seatwork directions with the whole class. Seatwork directions are written on the board. They include one or two assignments (such as journal writing) that students can do without any further explanation from the teacher. Groups one and three begin seatwork while the teacher meets with the middle spelling group for content development and more seatwork directions. The teacher then meets with the low group for checking and content development and gives them another assignment. She checks on the first group again before moving to content development with group three. In the time remaining in the period, after she finishes with the last group, she gives individual help to students and monitors seatwork.

An eighth-grade math teacher uses whole-class instruction for approximately the first half of the lessons in each chapter. Then students are divided into two groups: one containing six students and one with twenty-two students. The smaller group, which has students who are very deficient in math skills, uses a supplementary workbook covering essentially the same content and receives a second sequence of presentation, review, and practice similar to the material previously covered. The larger group continues in the textbook chapter until it has been completed.

Although small-group instruction can help cope with extreme heterogeneity, it presents more problems than modifying whole-class instruction. Small-group instruction makes classroom management and organization more difficult. It also requires more extensive planning and more materials—important considerations when you must prepare for five or six different class sections. Monitoring student behavior and work is more difficult because you are instructing the groups most of the period. Another important consideration is that when small-group instruction is used, students frequently spend relatively short periods of time interacting with you in content development and long periods of time in seatwork. Consequently, seatwork assignments have to be planned so that students will be able to do them with little assistance from the teacher. Despite all these problems, small-group instruction may sometimes be necessary to meet your students' needs, and it can be managed well with careful attention to instructional planning and classroom procedures. Some of the procedures you will have to decide on and explain to your students, if you use small-group instruction, are listed below.

Location of Group

Wherever you plan to meet, be sure that the location allows you to watch the rest of the class while you are working with the small group. Other considerations include minimizing distractions and making efficient use of classroom space and time.

Decide whether to rearrange student seating according to group or, if you have space in your room, whether you wish to set up a group instruction area. Rearranging seats by group has the advantage of eliminating student movement when you change groups; you move from one group to the other—the students need not leave their desks. Also, you may be able to plan small-group seating so that each group is close to a different board, screen, or display area for assignments and to different storage areas (for example, bookshelves) for materials. A disadvantage of rearranging seats according to small-group assignment is that it may have the effect of segregating students by achievement level and emphasizing differences among students. A good alternative, if you have the classroom space and workable numbers of students in each of your small groups, is to set up a table for small-group instruction at one end of your room.

Materials

You will have to plan for and obtain materials and supplies for each group and set up files or other storage facilities.

Student Movement

If you are able to set up a small-group instruction area to which you can call students, you will have to decide what procedures, rules, and signals you will use for student movement into and out of the group. Smooth and efficient transitions will depend on your explaining these procedures clearly and seeing that students follow them.

Out-of-Group Procedures

Before using group work you will need to communicate your expectations for students not in the group. For example:

- Will students be allowed to whisper or talk, or must they maintain silence?
- Under what circumstances may they leave their seats?
- What should they do if they need assistance on the assignment and you are not available?
- What should they do when they finish their work?

TEACHING LOW ACHIEVING CLASSES

In many secondary schools, especially in core academic subjects, students are assigned to classes on the basis of standardized test scores, academic record, teacher recommendations, diagnostic placement tests, or some combination of these factors. This process of homogeneous ability grouping or tracking results in the formation of several sections of a subject (for example, high, average, and low sections) or, at least, in special remedial classes for students deficient in basic skills. Such grouping practices are carried out on the assumption that they help schools provide instruction that meets the needs of all students. Many teachers and other educators believe that teaching and learning are more efficient when the range of achievement in a class is not too great. Unfortunately, concentrating lower achieving students in homogeneous groups often exacerbates management problems. When one is teaching a lower level class, poor classroom management and organization can result in a classroom climate in which any student would have difficulty learning. It is possible, however, to manage such classes effectively and to maintain student involvement in learning activities with little disruption. When such classes are effectively managed, students can make progress in the subject and complete the course with positive attitudes. Most of these students will do their work if they have a reasonable chance of success, and they will pay attention and cooperate with the teacher. However, obtaining good results with a lower track class is not an easy job. It requires extra effort both in managing behavior and in organizing instruction. The following paragraphs describe how to use that effort efficiently.

Learner Characteristics

Students in remedial classes usually are achieving two or more grade levels below average students at their grade and age levels. Their grades in the subject usually have been low in the past, and some may have failed the subject in a previous year. These students bring with them more than their share of problems, some resulting from their lower achievement and some contributing to lower achievement. For example, absence and tardiness are often higher in such classes. The completion rate for assignments, particularly for homework, is probably

"I'm an underachiever. . . .
What's your racket?"

lower than in average classes. Many low achieving students are likely to view grades as arbitrary, failing to see a connection between their classwork and homework and the grades they receive in a course. Frequent failure in school in the past has caused some of these students to become very discouraged, and they may react by giving up easily or by fighting back. Teachers may encounter these reactions in the extremes of apathy, belligerence, or clowning around in class. Some of these students will be very poor readers, which will cause them problems in all subject areas. Others may have poor memory abilities. Most have poor study skills (for example, in taking notes, outlining, being organized and methodical, pacing efforts on long-term assignments). Maintaining attention for long periods of time is often difficult, particularly when they encounter a demanding or frustrating task.

When considering these general characteristics, two important things should be kept in mind. First, a homogeneous low level class is not, of course, homogeneous at all. Such a class will contain students with a range of achievement levels, academic aptitudes, other talents, learning handicaps, goals and aspirations, attitudes toward school, and family backgrounds. Avoid making too many assumptions about individual students just because they have been placed in a low class. Second, the above description of general characteristics of students at low academic levels might be interpreted as a list of reasons why teaching such classes effectively is difficult (or impossible). It is not intended as such. Instead, it is intended as a description of needs that should be addressed by the management and organization plan for such a class. These general characteristics suggest some special considerations with regard to monitoring student behavior and work, establishing classroom procedures and rules, grading and accountability procedures, and organizing and presenting instruction.

Establishing Your Management System

In low track classes, particularly in the lower secondary grades, extra class time and attention may be required to teach students classroom procedures, rules, and routines at the beginning of the year. There may be more absences, shorter student attention spans, less ability to remember, and more testing of limits in such classes than in other class sections. Consequently, give extra attention to explaining, demonstrating, reviewing, and reminding students about your expectations; do not limit presentation, review, and feedback to only the first day or two of school. Plan to introduce and reinforce classroom procedures and routines gradually and methodically. Do not assume that students understand everything the first time you explain it. Question them, provide practice, and give them feedback. A "fun" written quiz on classroom procedures, routines, and requirements at the end of the first week of classes might be helpful. The following example illustrates how one junior high school teacher devoted part of class time throughout the first two weeks of school to establishing her management system in a lower track English class. After the first several weeks of school, the class was task-oriented and functioned smoothly.

On the first day of school, a Monday, Ms. Evans spent about twenty minutes discussing school and class rules with students in her low ability section. She described the rationale for each rule, and she explained the consequences of breaking rules. She also described a reward system for students who avoided detention hall during each six-week grading period. The discussion the first day was limited to basic school and class rules and procedures. Ms. Evans also described the routine to be used by the students at the beginning of class each day. She also told students what materials to bring to class, and she explained procedures they would use to turn in classwork.

On the second day of class, Ms. Evans devoted about twenty-one minutes to presenting additional procedures and reviewing some from the first day. As students entered the class, the teacher reminded them of the opening routine. After roll call she described and demonstrated the correct form for heading the daily assignment paper, and she circulated around the room to check that students were using it. Students then copied the school and class rules discussed on the first day of school onto a piece of paper for their notebooks. When they were finished with the seatwork assignment, the teacher discussed a rule that had not been discussed the first day and described course requirements and the grading system.

On the third day of class, Ms. Evans spent about six minutes discussing classroom rules, procedures, and routines with her students. Before the class started she reminded all the students of the beginning routine again. At the end of the class, she reviewed some of the school and class rules and procedures and reminded students that beginning the following day, penalties would be assessed for tardiness, failure to bring materials to class, and other rule violations.

On Friday, Ms. Evans devoted about ten minutes of class time to a discussion and review of procedures and rules. At the beginning of class, she did not remind the students about the beginning routine, but she monitored them closely and reminded two students who were slow to start it. Later she assigned a demerit to a student who failed to bring a pen or pencil, reviewing the reason for this procedure and penalty aloud to the class. At the end of the period, she conducted an informal oral quiz on class requirements, the grading system, and consequences for some rules and procedures. During the quiz she called on many different students rather than only on students who volunteered. After the quiz she praised the class for how successfully they had completed their first week of school in her class, and she talked with them during the final minutes of the period about their experiences at school during the week.

On the following Monday, the sixth day of school, Ms. Evans closely monitored the beginning class routine and prompted a few students who had forgotten it. She assigned a demerit to a student who failed to bring a pen or pencil. During the class, while students were engaged in a seatwork activity, there was an interruption from an outside visitor. After the visitor had left, the teacher reviewed her expectations for student behavior during interruptions. She also took this opportunity to review several other procedures and rules.

On the tenth day of class, Ms. Evans spent about fifteen minutes carefully explaining procedures that students would be using for a new activity: instruction, testing, and seatwork in three spelling groups. She assigned students to groups, explained rationales, and provided specific information about what the activity would involve, what she would be doing during group instruction, and what was expected of the students. She told students when spelling books were to be brought and reviewed the system she had set up for reminding students of materials needed for the next class period.

Monitoring Behavior

An absolutely essential ingredient of management is monitoring. You must be aware of what is occurring in your room. Keep your eyes on the students and scan the room frequently. If you see inappropriate behavior, deal with it promptly; when possible, use unobtrusive measures to stop it. Simple interventions such as eye contact or proximity to the students are best, as well as those that refocus the students' attention on their academic tasks. For example, "If you have questions about this work, raise your hand and I'll come help you," or "Bill, you should be working on the first five problems, not talking. When you finish number five, raise your hand and I will check your work." Prompt handling also minimizes the number of students involved and thus avoids creating peer pressure to resist the teacher or show off. Finally, you will give the correct impression of fairness and consistency in handling problems.

Managing Student Work

The cornerstone of an effective accountability system in lower level classes is an emphasis on daily and weekly grades. Such a system provides students with frequent feedback; it increases students' chances of success by making it difficult for individuals to fall far behind; it allows you to monitor student progress closely; and it helps develop good student work habits. Receiving some kind of grade or credit for effort and performance each day will help students accept responsibility for their schoolwork, especially if you have them keep a record sheet. You will need to allow time in class to show them how to follow this procedure. Have each student compute a weekly grade by calculating an average each week. Of course, you will have to teach them how to do this. Once established as a regular class procedure, it will help your students keep track of their progress. It will also make clear the effects of not completing one or more assignments during the week.

You should also consider making appropriate participation in class a part of your grading system. Participation includes answering when called on, volunteering questions, bringing appropriate materials to class, being on time, raising one's hand before speaking, and not calling out to other students or being out of ones's seat. Rewarding participation encourages involvement, learning, and attendance. There are several ways to include participation in your grading system. You can give weekly or daily points for each student to add to his or her daily assignment score. You can minimize bookkeeping time by giving participation scores as a closing activity. If your system is simple (for example, 3 points = good participation; 2 points = some; 1 point = a little; 0 = none, or disturbed class), you can award, record in your grade book, and call out points to twenty or so students in two or three minutes at the end of class.

You can also help make students accountable by making it clear that everyone is expected to participate in class discussions. To achieve this use some kind of system that will ensure that you call on every student at least once or twice. You might also keep a weekly answer sheet. Put each student's name on it and give checks for acceptable answers during recitation. You can then award points at the end of the week or when figuring weekly averages.

Planning and Presenting Instruction

In low ability classes more student learning and better classroom behavior are likely to result if (1) you organize classroom instruction into short activity segments with frequent assessments of student understanding, (2) you pay extra attention to presenting directions and instruction clearly, and (3) you build the teaching of study skills into your lessons. When planning classroom activities, avoid activity plans that require students to attend to a presentation or to work continuously for twenty-five or thirty minutes in the same seatwork activity. Instead, use two or more cycles of content development and student seatwork, as described and illustrated in Chapter 5 and in the case study of a mathematics lesson at the end of this chapter. There are two distinct advantages to using several cycles instead of one in lower ability classes. One advantage is that it is easier to maintain student involvement because of the shorter time segments. Another advantage is that by careful monitoring you can easily observe the extent to which students are able to complete the assignments. This will make it much easier to pace instruction appropriately and to give corrective feedback and repetition during a later content development activity.

When using several instructional cycles, you must be especially aware of two things: pacing and transitions. You will need to keep track of time in order to leave enough of it for each activity. One way to save enough time for later activities is to plan brief student assignments in the first (or the first and second) instructional cycle (for example, a few problems, exercises, questions, and so on) and to do one or two with the students to get them started. Thus, these earlier student assignments become somewhat extended work samples. To avoid confusion about the assignment, it is best to write it on the chalkboard or to display it on the overhead projector, even if it is quite short.

If a period contains more than one activity, it will have several transitions. Consequently, efficient transitions are a must. Rely on simple routines and use them very consistently. You might wish to review the discussion of transitions and pacing in Chapter 5.

Clear communication is important in all classes, but in lower ability classes clear directions and instruction are especially important; careless, overly complex communication is likely to result in student confusion, frustration, and misbehavior. Follow the guidelines for clarity discussed in Chapter 5, paying careful attention to the amount of information presented at one time, appropriate vocabulary, and the use of concrete or specific examples to illustrate new concepts. Check for student understanding frequently. Avoid overlapping many procedural directions. Get everyone's attention and then present directions in a step-by-step fashion, waiting for students to complete each step before going on the next. Finally, as you teach a lower ability class, be especially aware of opportunities to help your students improve their study and school survival skills. For example, assume that you must teach all your students how to take notes in your class. Provide demonstration, assistance, practice, monitoring, and feedback. Use content presentations or discussions of the text as vehicles for teaching students how

THE FAR SIDE   By GARY LARSON

to identify main ideas and supporting evidence. Include in your course some instructional activities that will help students build their vocabularies and improve their computation or memorization skills.

STUDENTS WITH SPECIAL NEEDS

This section deals with students who have special needs, either because they are physically or cognitively handicapped or because they have some characteristic that affects their classroom performance, such as limited language proficiency. Students with special needs who are identified as special education students are, by law, provided instruction in the least restrictive environment. As a result, more and more students with special needs are being served in the regular classroom with some outside help from specialized teachers. Meeting the needs of these students presents special challenges to teachers with a classroom full of other students. Fortunately, research has provided some specific guidelines to help teachers work with these students in ways that promote their peer acceptance and their self-esteem as well as their academic achievement. Following are some suggestions for planning instruction for students with different types of special needs.

Emotionally Disturbed Students

Remembering that emotionally disturbed students are usually different from others mainly in the degree of emotionality and their ability to regulate their behavior in response to those emotions rather than in the types of feelings they have may relieve some potential anxiety about working with them. If you have an emotionally disturbed student assigned to one of your classes, be sure to read the student's psychological report, if it is available to you (it must, of course, be treated confidentially), and note any recommendations for teachers. In addition, consult with the school psychologist, the student's parents, special education teachers, therapists, or anyone else who knows your student well, and find out how best to help the student succeed in your class.

If the emotionally disturbed student is one who has temper outbursts or becomes easily frustrated and angry, reinforce all attempts made toward self-control. Learn to recognize any behavioral cues that may precede an outburst so you can anticipate and intervene to prevent the student from losing control. Overlook minor inappropriate behavior, reinforce acceptable behavior, and reduce stressors, including lowering expectations temporarily if the student is having a bad day. Provide a supportive, predictable environment, offering the student structured choices when possible (e.g., Would you prefer to do the odd numbered problems or the even numbered? Would it be helpful for you to work at the table, or can you concentrate well enough at your own desk?). Work with your administrators and special education staff to devise a plan to carry out if an emotionally disturbed student becomes angry or aggressive. The student may need to be removed from the classroom to allow separation from other students with time to cool down. A safe time-out area should be designated for this purpose, and supervision should be continued during this time. If there is an adult on campus who has good rapport with the student, it would be helpful for that person to be available to talk with the student.

Remember that these students often do not know why they lose control, although they will frequently tend to blame something or someone outside themselves if required to explain. Helping them recognize the signs of increasing tension and offering them ways to defuse before they blow up increases their sense of control and self-esteem. After an outburst they may be embarrassed or remorseful, and it is important to reestablish your relationship with them once you and they are again calm. It is crucial that you not take personally their lack of cooperation, inappropriate behavior, or verbal attacks. If they lash out at you, remember that you are merely the convenient target, not the root cause of their pain and/or rage. Note, also, that students who frequently lose self-control are not good candidates for mainstreaming, and their status in a regular classroom should be reevaluated by the Admission, Review, and Dismissal Committee.

Attention-Deficit Hyperactivity Disordered Students

Broad characteristics of these students' behavior include distractibility, short attention spans, impulsiveness, an inability to organize, and a high level of movement. These symptoms vary in degree as well as combination. Some of these students will be mainly distractible and have short attention spans. Others will also be very impulsive and disorganized. When the features of the disorder are mild and when the student's academic skills are average or above average, the student is often able to compensate and to function reasonably well. When the student's academic abilities are weak and when the impulsive and distractible behaviors are frequent, then the student will experience considerable adjustment problems in most classrooms. It is important to remember that these behaviors are not deliberate and that it is very difficult and takes the student a long time to learn ways to compensate for or to control them. By the time they have reached middle or high school, many of these students have experienced much failure and have developed attitudes of discouragement and/or general negativism. A positive and low-key approach with much predictability and structure will help these students to function successfully. Talk with the student's previous teachers, parents, and special education teachers early in the year, if possible, to find out their ideas on what works best with the student.

When you give oral instructions, be sure you have the student's attention and make directions brief and clear. If a series of steps are involved, provide them in written form as well or have the student copy down the steps. Observe the student at the beginning of any new assignment and be willing to go over directions again individually. Remind the student that accuracy is more important than speed and encourage checking over work before handing it in. Allow the student to use a finger or a card as a marker when reading to avoid skipping words or lines.

Hearing Impaired Students

Students with a serious hearing loss may be able to function well in regular classes with minor modifications. Consult with a specialist for suggestions pertaining to your particular students. If adaptive devices are available (e.g., FM auditory system, caption decoders for videos), use them. Seat these students near the center of the room and close to the front. Always face the class when speaking; use the overhead projector rather than the chalkboard as you talk so that students can see your face while you are writing. Have the room well-lighted so these students can clearly see your lips and face to lip-read. Do not stand in front of windows or a bright doorway while talking; the glare behind you will make your face difficult to see.

Remember that understanding is more complex than just hearing or responding to a name, and these students may miss out on important information, being reluctant to ask you to repeat it. Use a routine of repeating and rephrasing important information or instructions and when possible, provide written directions. During class discussions, be sure to restate other students' questions and responses, since the hearing impaired students will probably not be able to lip-read these. Check frequently for understanding by asking these students a question during guided practice and closely monitoring as they begin written work. If note-taking is required, assign an able student with legible handwriting who is willing to take notes using carbon paper or who will provide a copy to the hearing impaired student. This is especially important during films. Hearing impaired students cannot take notes and lip-read at the same time. You can also assign a buddy to cue the hearing impaired student when it is important to watch the teacher or to locate information in the text.

Blind and Visually Impaired Students

Students who are blind or severely visually impaired may be able to function well in regular classes with your cooperation and help. Suggestions for adaptations of teaching methods and materials should be available in the functional visual assessment of the student written by a teacher of the visually impaired. In general, remember to verbalize anything that is written on the chalkboard or overhead projector. Allow students to use a tape recorder or to have fellow students make a copy of their notes for parents to read aloud at home. When possible, use tactile models along with verbal descriptions to demonstrate concepts. Encourage students to initiate a request for help when needed, and evaluate them using the same standards as for the rest of the class. If in doubt about how to help them, ask them directly, and do not be hesitant to discuss the vision problem with them. With students who have some vision, remember that although eyes cannot be strained from use, students may tire more quickly, in part because of the concentration and effort required to perceive and process from restricted stimuli. Allow students to hold printed material close to their eyes and to change the focus of activities frequently.

Students with Limited English Proficiency

There are many students in our schools for whom English is not their first language. Some of these students have acquired sufficient English language skills to perform successfully in English-only classes. Other students have not acquired a sufficient level of skill in speaking, understanding, reading, or writing English and need additional assistance to participate successfully in school activities. Some schools provide bilingual classes where school content is presented in the native language, and the student is provided assistance in learning English. Such classes may be provided only as the student makes the transition from exclusive use of a first language to use of English. Other schools provide English as a Second Language (ESL) classes, geared toward helping the student learn English as quickly as possible so that content learning can proceed in English. For many students, English learning occurs in conjunction with content learning in a regular classroom, sometimes with the aid of a language teacher or aide.

If you have students with limited English proficiency, find out from the bilingual or ESL teacher the extent of the students' production and understanding of English so your expectations will be fair and realistic. If the students' English skills are nonexistent, you will be better able to manage and instruct them if you learn some key words (e.g., "listen," "pay attention," "look") in the students' native language. Also learn what the students prefer to be called, and be sure to pronounce their names correctly. Rather than relying on someone to translate for you, use your creativity in communicating, speaking naturally and using pauses and many gestures. Reinforce key points with visual aids and demonstration when possible, and by repeating them in clear and concise words. A long receptive period is normal for students with limited proficiency in English, during which time they will respond with gestures, nods, etc., before they feel confident enough to speak any English words.

SUGGESTED ACTIVITIES

1. Chapter 2 includes a case study of procedures for small-group work in a science class. In addition to procedures for laboratory activities, the case study describes small-group discussion procedures that will help you in planning for the use of mixed-ability work groups in your class. Reread this case study.

2. Read Case Study 9–1, which details the procedures used by one English teacher for small-group instruction in spelling. As you read the case study, think about ways that these procedures might be adapted to your own classroom.

3. Read Case Study 9–2, which provides a good illustration of the use of several short content development–student seatwork cycles in a mathematics lesson in a lower level class.

4. Three scenarios at the end of this chapter describe problems frequently faced by teachers of heterogeneous or low ability classes. After reading each description, review appropriate parts of this and other chapters. Decide what strategies you would recommend to deal with the problems. Discuss each problem scenario with other teachers and make a brain-storming list of possible solutions and strategies. Afterward, compare your lists with those included in the keys in the Appendix.

CASE STUDY 9-1

USING SMALL GROUPS IN ENGLISH

Ms. Hanson uses small-group instruction during portions of each class period on two days a week for instruction and testing in spelling. On Tuesdays she meets with each of her three spelling groups for content development and introduction to seatwork on the new words for the week. Students in each group are seated together. This facilitates posting assignments, distributing or collecting papers, and group oral work.

The seatwork assignment for each group is posted near its area of the room. Each group's assignment includes at least one simple introductory task that students can do with no help from the teacher (for example, copying each word five times; looking up words in the dictionary and/or writing sentences with them). After the general instructions are given, all students begin work. The teacher works first with one group, going to its seating area to preview the words, work on pronunciation, and review the assignment. She then moves to another group.

During the group activity with Ms. Hanson, each student is included in some oral recitation.

At the end of the week, Ms. Hanson uses small groups to administer spelling tests. While students are entering the room, she tells them to get out their journals and prepare a sheet of paper for a spelling test. After the bell rings, the teacher introduces two activities which will be proceeding simultaneously: spelling tests for three groups and a composition assignment. She explains the composition (journal) assignment and then reminds the students that she will be going around the room administering spelling tests. When students are not taking the test, they are to work on the journal assignments. Students in each group are seated together. As the students begin work, the teacher begins administering the test to the first spelling group. She stands near the group's desks and uses a low voice. While she gives the test, she also monitors the rest of the class to make sure they remain on-task. After she finishes giving the test (about five minutes), the teacher collects the papers, puts them in a specially marked file folder and goes to the next group. She begins giving the test to the next group but continues to monitor the remainder of the class and signal for quiet when there is some noise from another area.

When the teacher finishes with the second group, she answers questions for students, files the papers, and then goes to the next group to give the test. She does not allow students to interrupt her while she is working with another group. When she finishes administering the test to the third spelling group, she collects the papers, files them, and lets the students know how much time they have to finish and to proof their journal assignment.

 ## CASE STUDY 9-2

MANAGING INSTRUCTION IN A LOWER LEVEL MATH CLASS

Time	Description	Activity
9:25	Mr. Washington begins a lesson on the addition of decimal numbers by describing the purpose of the lesson. He asks the review questions on decimals and place value, and he gives several examples using money—dollars and cents. He then puts an addition problem on the chalkboard. The numbers are written on one line (horizontally) and have the same number of place values after the decimal point. He reminds the class that adding decimals is similar to adding	Content development

(Continued)

Time	Description	Activity
	whole numbers, but that students must copy the numbers into a column (up and down), being sure that the decimal points are on a straight line (each one above or below the others). They must also be very careful to copy the numbers correctly. He then recopies the problem as column addition, discussing the steps, and tells students to copy the examples. He looks at their work, complimenting them when they copy correctly. He calls on students to perform the addition for the problems and reminds them to be sure to put the decimal in the correct position in the answer. He again uses examples of dollars and cents in order to show the effect of errors and to emphasize the importance of the lesson. Next Mr. Washington puts another example on the board and calls on a student to work it. Edward tries to work through the problem and then says, "Tell me what's wrong!" The teacher says, "Well, let's find out. How can we tell?" The teacher and the class then work through the problem again.	
9:38	The teacher then displays three new problems on the overhead projector and asks the students to work the problems on the paper they will be using for the assignment. As the students are working, Mr. Washington circulates, checking to see if the students are doing the problems correctly. He sees one student who has moved the decimal point in some numbers, and he says to the class, "Check to be sure you've copied the problem correctly before you add."	Classwork—with teacher monitoring and feedback
9:42	After most of the students have completed the problems, the teacher stops them and says, "Let's look up here." He then introduces addition problems having different numbers of decimal place values. He work one, explaining how it is similar to and different from the earlier problems. He does two more examples with the class,	Content development, work sample

Time	Description	Activity
	describing or asking students to describe each step. Mr. Washington then tells students that he is going to do a problem incorrectly and that they should try to catch his mistakes. Afterwards, he and the class do one more example step by step. Then he displays another problem on the overhead projector and directs students to work on it on their papers. Circulating around the room, he sees that all can do it.	
10:00	After discussing the problem, the teacher gives an assignment orally and also writes it on the board. He has the student copy the assignment onto their papers and begin work. As the students work he walks around, checking on their progress and helping them when necessary. The students work quietly, and the teacher continues to help them throughout the activity.	Seatwork assignment, monitoring
10:19	One minute before the end of class, Mr. Washington brings the activity to a close, reminds students that the assignment is due tomorrow at the beginning of class, and then makes some general announcements before the bell rings at 10:20. When the bell rings, he dismisses the class.	Closing

 PROBLEM 9-1

HETEROGENEOUS CLASSES

Never before has Ms. Rogers had to deal with students of such different entering achievement levels in her seventh-grade class. She feels frustrated in her efforts to provide instruction at appropriate levels for some students several years below grade level and others above grade level. The brightest students finish seatwork far ahead of the rest of the class, while the slowest students seldom complete an assignment successfully.

So far Ms. Rogers has tried two things. She decided to provide extra-credit activities for students who finish work early, and she has begun to help slower students individually more often during class and after school. Both of these steps seem to help, although each has also created some management problems. What additional things might Ms. Rogers do?

? PROBLEM 9-2

TEACHING A LOWER LEVEL CLASS

Sometimes Ms. Porter feels that the students in her low ability second-period class are either unwilling or unable to learn anything. Many seem apathetic; they won't even try. Many have short attention spans, and some seem to require constant individual assistance.

At the beginning of the year, Ms. Porter assumed that she would teach her lower section much as she would teach the other classes, except for using a slower pace and allowing more practice and drill for the students. After several weeks of school, she realized that other adjustments would have to be made as well. She began showing students exactly what to write down for notes during teacher presentations, and she began asking more frequent, simple review questions in class to hold students' attention and help them learn. These measures helped, but many students still don't complete their work successfully. What are some other adjustments Ms. Porter might make?

? PROBLEM 9-3

STUDENT BEHAVIOR IN A LOWER LEVEL CLASS

Mr. Oliver is concerned about behavior in his lower level class. Several students are always late while others frequently forget their books, paper, pencils, or assignments. During content presentations students call out answers or comments, leave their seats to throw away paper or sharpen their pencils, and they often talk or write notes. During seatwork assignments students work the first problem or two while teacher is watching but then turn to their neighbors as soon as the teacher turns his back to work with individual students. Mr. Oliver tried to establish order by using a fine system, in which students had to write out and turn in definitions of problems if they were caught misbehaving. This system had worked well with his average classes, but in this class he found he was constantly handing out fines and was unable to keep track of whether they were turned in. What other ideas could Mr. Oliver try?

Appendix: Answer Keys for Chapter Activities

CHAPTER 1

Activity 1

The room arrangement shown in Figure 1-2 will contribute to classroom management problems in a number of ways. Specific items are listed below.

- Students at the rear of the the row furthest left will have difficulty seeing the overhead projector screen.
- When the teacher stands at the overhead projector, six students will be seated behind her.
- Desks are arranged so that students face other students. Although this formation may be useful during class discussions for encouraging students to respond to each other, it may produce a high level of distraction during other activities.
- Some student desks face windows, which might also be a source of distraction. These same desks face away from a chalkboard.
- The group of four desks on the right-hand side of the room is in front of the bookshelf and impedes movement in that area of the room. Students at those desks are likely to be distracted by students using materials or equipment at that end of the room.
- The wastebasket is not conveniently located; a place nearer the door would be better.
- The table is too near the teacher's desk and crowds several student desks.
- Students working at the table might disturb others nearby. Traffic flow in the area around the teacher's desk and table is poor.
- The major instructional area by the overhead projector has no table, desk, or other storage space to hold materials needed in presentations.

CHAPTER 3

Case Study 3-4

Diagnosis

Ms. Wood has problems keeping her general mathematics students responsible for their work assignments. In her algebra classes, where students are more motivated, Ms. Wood has fewer problems. Her general mathematics students, however, may need help in learning to assemble a notebook, becoming responsible for doing quality work and for completing it. Because 75 percent of their grade is based on tests, and because their daily work is checked only once a week, students probably think that their daily work is not very important. This has probably contributed to their poor sense of responsibility.

Suggestions

Ms. Wood should review her accountability procedures and her grading system, giving consideration to the following items.

- Make certain all students know how each assignment contributes to their overall grade and that instructions are clear with respect to completeness, neatness, quality of work, and due dates.
- Monitor progress frequently once standards have been established and students understand them. Students should receive regular feedback.
- Check notebooks periodically for completeness, thus keeping students from getting too far behind.
- Be explicit about what is to be included in the notebooks and how it should be organized. Notebooks should also contain a table of contents and a list of required assignments. Displaying a model notebook would be helpful.
- Allow students to check their own assignments or to exchange papers. This will help provide immediate feedback, and it will allow for more frequent checking of required work.
- Have students keep track of their daily grades, quizzes, and extra-credit work. Spend some class time helping them compute averages on different occasions during the grading period.
- As students work, circulate and monitor student progress rather than remain at the teacher's desk.
- Check promptly with students who fail to turn in assignments. If students need help, provide it; otherwise, require that assignments be completed.
- Do a portion of each assignment orally and question students to check for understanding.

CHAPTER 4

Case Study 4-4

Diagnosis

Mr. Davis has failed to be specific with his students about his expectations for their behavior. His only rule is too general to serve for all situations. Because he used one general rule, Mr. Davis must constantly interpret concrete instances of infractions as they relate to the rule. Furthermore, he has not been specific about consequences and has mentioned only one penalty, that of going to the office. Mild misbehaviors at the beginning of the year have now escalated into more serious misbehaviors as students test the limits. At this stage Mr. Davis is receiving poor cooperation both in obtaining written work from students and in the area of class participation.

Suggestions

Mr. Davis might begin to establish better behavior in his class in the following ways.

- Reevaluate the rules and procedures with the intent of making them more specific, and introduce rules and procedures for areas that were previously not covered.

- Select a time such as a Monday or the day after a vacation period to reintroduce and explain the rules and procedures, providing students with rationales for the desired behaviors and eliciting their cooperation in following them.

- Review procedures for participating in class discussions and for those times when whispering and working together is allowed and when it is not.

- Once the rules and procedures are introduced, clear and specific consequences for infractions should be stated. These should be tied to the behaviors themselves; trips to the office should be used only for the most serious offenses. Positive as well as negative consequences should be considered and communicated to students.

- Monitor the class constantly with the goal of anticipating and preventing misbehavior and noting appropriate behavior.

- Make sure that students have enough work to do and that they understand it and are able to complete it. Require student attention during presentations and allow only relevant materials and books to be out on desks. Have students take notes during important parts of the presentation: Be explicit and teach them how to take notes. Require these as part of a notebook.

- Break longer activities into shorter ones and vary the sequencing and routine for the sixth-period class. Students are tired at this time of the day and maintaining attention is not easy even with well-behaved classes.

- Pace students through their work with statements such as, "You should be halfway through with this assignment by now," or "We will check the first part of the assignment in five minutes."

- Reward academic performance and other desirable classroom behavior regularly. For students of this age, extra-credit points or privileges may be more reinforcing then public praise.

CHAPTER 5

Case Study 5-1

The following suggestions for Ms. Carpenter would help improve her students' comprehension.

- Outline the lesson sequence, breaking down complex lessons into smaller, easier-to-understand parts or steps. Be sure to define words that students may not know.

- During presentations let students know what they are expected to write in their notes by underlining important points as they are written on the chalkboard, or by displaying them on an overhead projector transparency. Another way to structure note taking is to give students an outline with space for additional notes.

- During content development activities obtain frequent work samples by having students do problems or answer questions. Circulate during these times, checking for areas of confusion, common problems, and students who are not participating. Based on feedback from these samples, adjust instruction either by slowing down, by increasing the pace of the presentation, or by repeating content where necessary.

- Be sure students know the purpose of the lesson, and at the end of presentations, always restate major objectives or else quiz students on important points.

- Give students step-by-step instructions for assignments. Check to be sure they understand what they are to do, and then help them pace their work by telling them how long the assignment should take to complete and warning them when there is a short time left.

- Circulate while students are doing seatwork assignments. Check to be sure they are working on the assignment, that they are doing it correctly, and that they are using their time wisely.

- If it becomes apparent during a seatwork or recitation activity that some students do not understand the material, have them join you in a small group after the general presentation. At this time you can review the points of the lesson and answer questions.

CHAPTER 5

Case Study 5-2

Mr. Miller could reduce the amount of time wasted by his class if he would use the following approaches.

- Use an academic warmup as part of the beginning-of-class routine. Have the warmup written on the chalkboard or displayed on an overhead transparency, and require that students complete the task in a set period of time (for example, five minutes). Be sure that warmup activities are checked and that they count toward the students' grades.
- Use established routines as much as possible for beginning and ending lessons, passing and collecting papers and supplies, and exchanging papers to grade. Monitor to be sure students follow routines.
- Teach students exactly what behaviors are expected during transitions: voice level, pencil sharpener use, procedures for passing papers, and so on.
- Give instructions for what is to be done before beginning transitions, not during them.
- Post assignments where all students can see them. Begin seatwork assignments together as a class, doing the first problems or answering the first question as a group. Then monitor at the beginning of seatwork to be sure everyone gets off to a good start.

CHAPTER 5

Case Study 5-3

Ms. Kendall could begin organizing her curriculum for the year by taking the following steps.

- Seek out existing curriculum guides. Check with the department chairperson for copies of system-wide curricula, goals, and objectives, as well as anything that is unique to her school. Obtain a copy of the teachers' manual for the text and examine the suggested yearly outline. Seek out the suggestions and aid of a successful teacher who has taught the class for several years and is willing to share ideas and materials. Call the school system's science coordinator for additional information and to find out what resources are available.

- Before preparing lesson plans, gather information on students, texts, facilities, and budget. How many students will be in the class and what are their ability levels and prior science courses? What books will be used and will sufficient quantities be on hand when the school year begins? What facilities, equipment, and materials will be available? What may be purchased and how are requisitions handled?

- Refer to the lesson plan guidelines set forth in Chapter 5. Be sure to include a variety of activities each day—no lesson should be straight lecture or all seatwork. During the first week, allow more time for emphasis on student learning of rules and procedures. Teach students how to participate appropriately in class, and gear the first week's academic activities to student success. Also, during the first several weeks be sure to set in place procedures for developing student accountability (refer to Chapter 3).

CHAPTER 5

Case Study 5-4

As his fourth-period class begins, Mr. Case makes eye contact with two students who are exchanging notes; the students quickly get out their class materials. **(Withitness.)** "Let's begin by working some of the exercises at the end of the chapter; you'll need your notebooks." As students begin to get out their materials, Mr. Case calls out, "Oops, I forgot to tell you to bring money tomorrow for the field trip. How many of you will be going?" **(Thrust.)** After a brief discussion, students finish getting out their materials. Mr. Case says, "We'll go through these exercises orally, but I also want you to write the answers in your notebooks as part of today's classwork. I'll come around and check your notebook work later in the period. **(High participation format and accountability.)** Now who can answer the first question? Hands please. Tyrone?" Mr. Case conducts the lesson by calling on various students, some with hands up, others seemingly at random from the nonvolunteers. **(Group alerting.)** About halfway through the exercises, a student enters the room and says that he is new to the school and has been assigned to the class. Mr. Case goes to his desk, sits down, and says, "OK, come here. I'll check out a text to you. **(Absence of overlapping.)** I wish the school office wouldn't send people in the middle of the period. Where are you from anyway?" **(Stimulus-boundedness.)** After giving the student a syllabus and a text, Mr. Case leaves his desk and says to the class, "Now where were we? Oh yes, question 7. Say, where did Kim and Lee go? I didn't give them permission to leave." **(Absence of withitness.)** After several minutes more, Mr. Case calls a halt to the activity and says, "Now I'd like us to discuss the test coming up this Thursday. Let's make sure that you are all clear on what will be on the exam and what you will need to study to get ready for it." After a pause, he adds: "I almost forgot. Get out your questions from before and look at the next to the last one. We need to add an important point that was left out . . ." After finishing the item, Mr. Case turns the topic back to the upcoming test. **(Flip-flop.)** Now, where were we? Oh yes, I need to show you some items that will be similar to those on the test. Here's one." He writes it on the chalkboard, then pauses: "Well, I don't want to give away the test, do I?" Without discussing the test further, he turns to another topic. **(Dangle.)** "Just wait until you hear about the videotape we will be viewing tomorrow. I borrowed it from another teacher and she said that her students thought it was one of the most thought-provoking, exciting stories they had ever seen!" **(Group alerting.)**

CHAPTER 5

Case Study 5-5

Diagnosis

Ms. Grant has made a common mistake. She assumes that students will be able to follow her directions with a minimum of structuring or explanation on her part. In this case study she assigns lab work that requires students to work in groups but does not prepare them for this activity. Group assignments are handed out but not explained clearly, nor do students attend to the directions. When students move to their groups, transitions are disorderly, and once in the groups, directions are vague as to how students are to pursue the question, "What is in the box?" The activity drags, and several groups sit in dead time while others finish. Groups are expected to report their findings, but no directions are given about how to do this. At the end of the activity, Ms. Grant provides no wrap-up or evaluation, and she assigns a textbook reading on a different topic.

Suggestions

Ms. Grant might achieve more success with her class if she presents information systematically. The following items will help.

- State major goals and objectives and let students know what they will be responsible for knowing.
- Call for attention and do not proceed without it. Require that students listen to directions and presentations. Have them respond to questions and demonstrations.
- Explain precisely what behaviors are expected when students work together in groups on an assignment. At the same time, groups should pick a recorder

who will be responsible for presenting the group reports to the rest of the class.

- As groups are working, monitor and circulate to make certain they are on the right track. If widespread problems seem to be occurring, reteach the material. Allow students to begin work only when satisfied that they can complete the tasks satisfactorily.

- Provide additional activities for groups who finish early so that unnecessary dead time is avoided.

- Constructively evaluate the individual reports rather than accepting poor or incomplete answers.

- Follow up the group activity with relevant discussion and a summary of the lesson.

CHAPTER 7

Activity 7-2

1. b   2. c   3. d   4. a   5. c

CHAPTER 9

Problem 9-1

To deal with very diverse ability levels, Ms. Rogers might try the following approaches.

- If one or two students are especially likely to have trouble with whole-class assignments, these students can be seated where the teacher can easily keep an eye on them during instruction and seatwork. As soon as seatwork instructions have been given to the whole class and the teacher has monitored to be sure they have begun work, she can check with slower students privately to go over instructions again or to modify the assignment, as necessary. These instructions and directions can be done as a small-group activity if more than one or two students need the extra assistance.

- Enrichment or extra-credit material for students who finish classwork early should include work-related activities that will not distract other students. Feedback, credit, and recognition for completion of enrichment activities should be a part of the system.

- All students in the class should be involved in discussion or recitation sessions. Systematically calling on each student will give everyone an opportunity to participate.

- If the above suggestions are not sufficient for a given class, small-group instruction might be used for part of the course work. Procedures for group work must be planned, then taught carefully. When two or three work groups are established in a class, instruction and monitoring will be simpler if seat-work assignments are planned so that there is a basic assignment that all students do, with additional activities at appropriate levels for each group. Some of the instruction can then be with the whole class, while a smaller amount can be reserved for each group.

- When using differentiated assignments, adjustments in the grading system should be made so that lower-ability students can attain satisfactory grades.

CHAPTER 9

Problem 9-2

If she is not already doing so, Ms. Porter should be sure that she is spending adequate class time explaining the material to the whole class. This is preferable to trying to impart the instruction to individuals during seatwork. To avoid long presentations and the attendant problem of maintaining student attention and participation, divide the presentation into two (or more) segments, with short periods of seatwork or classwork in between.

- Frequent work samples, written as well as oral, should be obtained from students during content development activities to keep abreast of student understanding.

- Every student should be included in discussions or recitations to keep them involved in the activity.

- Providing structure for classwork and homework is essential. All assignments in class should be begun as a group exercise. Dittos or worksheets that lead students through tasks in a step-by-step fashion with frequent, short written responses also are helpful.

- Daily grades should be emphasized, and students should be provided with frequent feedback about their progress to support and encourage their efforts.

CHAPTER 9

Problem 9-3

Mr. Oliver should reconsider his classroom rules and procedures to determine whether they cover the misbehaviors that are causing him a problem. If adjustments are needed, the relevant rule or procedure should be restated and introduced to the students again. Mr. Oliver should also consider whether his monitoring is adequate or whether students are getting away with too much misbehavior before he deals with the problem. In addition, some measures to correct or prevent specific problems described in the case study are listed below.

- Mr. Oliver may be overrelying on the fine system to respond to misbehavior. If so, it would be better to use such penalties only for a limited number of situations (for example, forgetting materials or disturbing the class). Recording fines can be simplified by keeping a clipboard with a list of students' names and a place for a daily record.

- Compliance with procedures can be rewarded by awarding points toward grades. Give students daily points or checks for having appropriate materials, being in their seats and ready to work when the bell rings, and staying on task throughout the period.

- There are several ways to help students remember to bring materials. A supply of pens or pencils may be kept on hand for emergency loans, with some penalty imposed when students have to borrow supplies. Students can be allowed to leave pencils and papers in the classroom so that they will always be available. These can be labeled or kept in a folder with the students' names and class period listed on it. If different materials are needed on different days, Mr. Oliver could have students keep a record of materials and assignments needed for the class so that they can refer to it as necessary. He could also post a list of books and other materials above or next to the door so that students could see it before they enter the room.

- Before content presentations Mr. Oliver might remind students that he will call on them to answer and that they should not call out except when he signals that it is appropriate.

- Inappropriate behavior during presentations should be stopped by a simple procedure, such as eye contact or reminding students of the procedure or rule, without interfering with the flow of the lesson. If the behavior persists, a penalty can be imposed.

- It is always helpful to move around the room during presentations and while students are engaged in seatwork activities. Mr. Oliver should walk by every student in the room, looking at papers to be sure that students are working on the right assignment and doing it correctly. He should avoid staying too long with any one student, and if a student needs additional help, he or she can come to a table or desk from which Mr. Oliver can monitor all the students. Frequent circulating will tend to discourage note writers and talkers.

References and
Further Readings

Alberti, R. L., ed. (1977). *Assertiveness: Innovations, applications, issues.* San Luis Obispo, Calif: Impact Publishers.

Bandura, A. (1986). *Social foundations of thought and action.* Englewood Cliffs, N.J.: Prentice-Hall, Inc.

Bassin, A., Bratter, E., & Ruchin, R., eds. (1976). *The Reality Therapy reader: A survey of the works of William Glasser.* New York: Harper & Row.

Brophy, J. E. (1981). Teacher praise: A functional analysis. *Review of Educational Research, 51,* 5–32.

Canter, L., & Canter, M. (1976). *Assertive discipline.* Santa Monica, Calif.: Canter and Associates, Inc.

Canter, L. (1989) *Assertive discipline for secondary educators.* Santa Monica, Calif.: Canter and Associates, Inc.

Clements, B. S., & Evertson, C. M. (1982). *Orchestrating small group instruction in elementary school classrooms.* Austin, Texas: Research and Development Center for Teacher Education. Report No. 6053. (ERIC Document Reproduction Service No. ED 251 433).

Deci, E. L., & Ryan, R. M. (1985). *Intrinsic motivation and self-determination in human behavior.* New York: Plenum Press.

Doyle, W. (1986). Classroom organization and management. In M. C. Wittrock, ed., *Handbook of research on teaching* (3rd ed.). New York: Macmillan.

Dreikurs, R., Grunwald, B., & Pepper, F. (1982). *Maintaining sanity in the classroom: Classroom management techniques* (2nd ed.). New York: Harper & Row.

Duke, D. L., ed. (1979). *Classroom management. The 78th yearbook of the National Society for the Study of Education, Part II.* Chicago: University of Chicago Press.

Duke, D. L., ed. (1982). *Helping teachers manage classrooms.* Alexandria, Va.: Association for Supervision and Curriculum Development.

Emmer, E. T. (1986). Academic activities and tasks in first-year teachers' classes. *Teaching and Teacher Education, 2,* 229–244.

Emmer, E. T. (1987). Classroom management and discipline. In V. Richardson-Koehler, ed. *Educators' handbook: A research perspective.* New York: Longman.

Emmer, E. T. (1988). Praise and the instructional process. *Journal of Classroom Interaction,* *23,* 32–39.

Emmer, E. & Aussiker, A. (1990). School and classroom discipline programs: How well do they work? In O. Moles, ed. *Student discipline strategies: Research and practice.* Albany, N.Y.: SUNY Press.

Emmer, E. T., & Evertson, C. M. (1981). Synthesis of research on classroom management. *Educational Leadership, 38,* 342–347.

Emmer, E. T., Evertson, C. M., & Anderson, L. M. (1980). Effective classroom management at the beginning of the school year. *Elementary School Journal, 80,* 219–231.

Evertson, C. M. (1982). Differences in instructional activities in higher and lower achieving junior high English and math classes. *The Elementary School Journal, 82,* 329–350.

Evertson, C. M. (1985). Training teachers in classroom management. An experimental study in secondary school classrooms. *Journal of Educational Research, 79,* 51–58.

Evertson, C. M. (1987). Managing classrooms: A framework for teachers. In D. Berliner & B. Rosenshine, eds. *Talks to Teachers.* New York: Random House.

Evertson, C. M., & Emmer, E. T. (1982). Effective management at the beginning of the school year in junior high classes. *Journal of Educational Psychology, 74,* 485–498.

Evertson, C. M., Emmer, E., Clements, B., & Worsham, M. (1994). *Classroom management for elementary teachers* (3rd ed.). Boston: Allyn and Bacon.

Evertson, C. M., Sanford, J. P., & Emmer, E. T. (1981). Effects of class heterogeneity in junior high school. *American Educational Research Association, 18,* 219–232.

Evertson, C. M., & Weade, R. (1989). Classroom management and teaching style: Instructional stability and variability of two junior high English classrooms. *Elementary School Journal, 89,* 379–393.

Foster, H. L. (1986). *Ribbin', jivin', and playin' the dozens: The persistent dilemma in our schools* (2nd ed.). Cambridge, Mass.: Ballinger Publishing Co.

Gazda, G., et al. (1977). *Human relations development: A manual for educators* (2nd ed.). Boston: Allyn and Bacon.

Glasser, W. (1975). *Reality Therapy: A new approach to psychiatry.* New York: Harper & Row.

Glasser, W. (1977). 10 steps to good discipline. *Today's Education, 66,* 60–63.

Glasser, W. (1986). *Control theory in the classroom.* New York: Harper & Row.

Good, T. L., & Brophy, J. E. (1987). *Looking in classrooms* (4th ed.). New York: Harper & Row.

Gordon, T. (1974). *Teacher effectiveness training.* New York: Peter H. Wyden.

Johnson, D. W., & Johnson, R. T. (1987). *Learning together and alone: Cooperative, competitive, and individualistic learning.* (2nd ed.). Englewood Cliffs, N.J.: Prentice-Hall.

Jones, V., & Jones, L. (1990). *Comprehensive classroom management: Motivating and managing students.* (3rd ed.) Boston: Allyn & Bacon.

Kounin, J. S. (1970). *Discipline and group management in classrooms.* New York: Holt, Rinehart & Winston.

Kounin, J. S., & GUMP, P. (1974). Signal systems of lesson settings and the task related behavior of preschool children. *Journal of Educational Psychology, 66,* 554–562.

Kounin, J. S., & Obradovic, S. (1968). Managing emotionally disturbed children in regular classrooms: A replication and extension. *Journal of Special Education, 2,* 129–135.

Lepper, M. R., & Greene, D. eds. (1978). *The hidden costs of reward: New perspectives on the psychology of human motivation.* Hillsdale, N.J.: Erlbaum.

Pitcher, G., & Poland, S. (1992). *Crisis intervention in the schools.* New York: Guilford Press.

Sanford, J. P., & Emmer, E. T. (1988). *Understanding classroom management: An observation guide.* Englewood Cliffs, N.J.: Prentice-Hall.

Sanford, J. P., Emmer, E. T., & Clements, B. S. (1983). Improving classroom management. *Educational Leadership, 40,* 56–61.

Sanford, J. P., & Evertson, C. M. (1981). Classroom management in a low SES junior high: Three case studies. *Journal of Teacher Education, 32*(1), 34–38.

Slavin, R. E. (1990). *Cooperative learning: Theory, research, and practice.* Englewood Cliffs, N.J.: Prentice-Hall.

Slavin, R. E. (1991). *Student team learning: A practical guide to cooperative learning* (3rd ed.). Washington, D.C.: NEA Professional Library.

Slavin, R., Sharan, S., Kagan, S., Hertz-Lazarowitz, R., Webb, C., & Schmuck, R., eds. (1985). *Learning to cooperate, cooperating to learn.* New York: Plenum.

Stoner, G., Shinn, M., & Walker, H. (1991). *Interventions for achievement and behavior problems.* Silver Spring, Md.: National Association of School Psychologists.

Zuker, E. (1983). *Mastering assertiveness skills: Power and positive influence at work.* New York: AMACOM.

INDEX